DELHI FORT

A GUIDE TO THE BUILDINGS AND GARDENS

DELHI FORT

A GUIDE TO THE BUILDINGS AND GARDENS

GORDON SANDERSON
Maulvi Shuaib

GYAN

Published by

GYAN

Gyan Publishing House
5, Ansari Road
Daryaganj, New Delhi-110002
Phone: 011-47034999, 9811692060
E-mail: books@gyanbooks.com

Distribution Network
gyanbooks.com
India, USA, Canada, UK, Australia, France

ISBN : 9788121232999 (PB)
First Published, Delhi, 1914

2nd Impression 2020

Printed at: Gyan Press, Delhi.

Delhi Fort
A Guide to the Buildings and Gardens
Author: Gordon Sanderson

A GUIDE TO THE BUILDINGS AND GARDENS

DELHI FORT

"SHAHJAHAN'S GREATEST SPLENDOUR WAS SHOWN IN HIS BUILDINGS"

ELPHINSTONE

DELHI: MANAGER OF PUBLICATIONS
1937

PREFACE TO THE SECOND EDITION.

LITTLE has to be added to the first edition compiled by the late Mr. G. Sanderson in 1914. A few details of subsequent expenditure on the conservation of the fort palaces have been given in the summary of archæological work carried out appearing at the end of the book; but the bulk of this work was done between the years 1903-12. A few typographical errors have been corrected, and the transliteration of Persian names into English characters has been made to conform with the system now generally adopted on the recommendations of the International Oriental Congress of 1894.

J. A. PAGE, A.R.I.B.A.,
Superintendent,
Muhammadan and British Monuments,
Northern Circle, Agra.

May 1918.

PREFACE TO THE THIRD EDITION.

THIS edition is a reprint of the previous one. Opportunity has also been taken of correcting a few errors and bringing the expenditure on the conservation of the Fort Palaces up-to-date.

My assistant Maulvi Ashraf Husain, B.A., has been of considerable help in checking the references.

B. L. DHAMA,

Offg. Superintendent,
Muhammadan and British Monuments,
Northern Circle, Agra.

August 1928.

PREFACE TO THE FOURTH EDITION.

THIS edition is also a reprint of the previous one with minor modifications. The expenditure on the conservation of the Fort Palaces has again been brought up-to-date.

ZAFAR HASAN,
Superintendent, Archæological Survey, Northern Circle, Agra.

Reprint—1936.

INTRODUCTION.

THE following notes are an attempt to combine all that is of chief interest in the numerous works, a list of which will be found overleaf, that refer to the Palace of Shāhjahān at Delhi, in the hope that they may lend an added interest to a visit to the Fort. The information from Indian historians has been collected by the late Maulvi Shuaib, formerly a member of my staff. It has been somewhat difficult to keep the notes within the scope of what is generally known as a "guide" and the writer hopes that the text will not be found to be overloaded with quotations. Some of these are, however, of considerable interest and local colour, and throw much additional light on the history of the buildings and their former functions. The plan is taken from the reproduction of the old plan of the Fort illustrated in Fergusson's *History of Eastern and Indian Architecture.* It contains several rather prominent inaccuracies but gives, on the whole, a fairly good idea of the former arrangement of the interior of the Palace. The measurements on the plan have been added by the writer for purpose of reference. It is suggested that the "birds-eye" sketch, which is an attempt at the conjectural restoration of the Palace buildings as they stood in the days of the "Great Mogul," be studied with the plan. The translations of the inscriptions on the Khwābgāh and Muthāmmān Burj have been given by Maulvi Zafar Hasan, Assistant Superintendent, Northern Circle.

GORDON SANDERSON,

Superintendent,
Muhammadan and British Monuments,
Northern Circle.

April 1914.

CONTENTS.

PAGE.

The Fort, its Foundation and cost	1
The Lahore and Delhi gates	8
The other gates	11
Chhatta Chauk (vaulted arcade from the Lahore gate to the Naubat Khana)	12
Naubat or Naqqar Khana	14
Diwan-i-Amm	15
Mumtaz Mahal	26
Rang Mahal	28
Marble Basin	31
Tasbih Khana, Khwabgah, and Baithak	35
Muthamman Burj	38
Diwan-i-Khass	41
Peacock Throne	46
Hammam	53
Moti Masjid	55
Hira Mahal	57
Shah Burj	*ibid*
Asad Burj	59
Hayat Bakhsh Garden	60
The Sawan and Bhadon pavilions	61
The Nahr-i-Bihisht	63
Salimgarh	65
The Fort during the Mutiny	68
Archæological work carried out in the Fort	82

LIST OF AUTHORITIES CITED.

Archæology of Delhi. Carr Stephen. Calcutta; Thacker, Spink & Co., 1876.

Archæological Survey of India Annual, 1902-1910.

Archæological Survey of India Reports, Cunningham.

Asiatic Researches, London, 1807.

Catalogue, Delhi Museum of Archæology (1909-Ed.), J. Ph. Vogel. Calcutta, Baptist Mission Press; (1913-Ed.), Gordon Sanderson, Government Press, Calcutta.

Delhi Past and Present, H. C. Fanshawe. London; John Murray, 1902.

Fall of the Moghul Empire, H. G. Keene. London, Allen & Co., 1887.

Guide to Delhi, H. G. Keene. Calcutta; Thacker, Spink & Co., 1906.

Handbook for Delhi, Fredrick Cooper. Lahore Chronicle Press, 1865.

History of Eastern and Indian Architecture, James Fergusson (revised by Burgess and Spiers). London; John Murray, 1910.

History of the Great Moghuls, Pringle Kennedy. Calcutta; Thacker, Spink & Co., 1911.

Imperial India, Prinsep. London; Chapman & Hall.

India through the Ages, F. A. Steel. London; Routledge & Sons, 1908.

Indian Mutiny papers.

Journal of a tour in India, General Mundy. London; John Murray, 1858.

Journal of a tour in Upper India, C. T. French. Simla, 1872.

Journey through India, Reginald Heber. London; John Murray, 1828.

Memoirs of Delhi and Fyzabad, Hoey. Allahabad, 1889.

New guide to Delhi, Harcourt. Meerut, 1870.

Oriental Annual (1835—1840), T. Bacon. London; Charles Tilt, 1840.

Oriental Biographical Dictionary, T. W. Beale. London; 1904.

Persia and the Persian Question. Hon. G. Curzon, M. P., London: 1892.

Proceedings of trial of Muhammad Bahadur Shah, 27th January 1858 and following days. Calcutta Government Press, 1895.

Rambles and Recollections of an Indian Official, Sleeman. London; Hatchard & Son, 1844.

Reports of the Curator of Ancient Monuments in India, Volumes I, II, III.

Sale's translation of the Koran. London; 1857.

Scenes and characteristics of Hindustan, Emma Roberts. London; Allen & Co., 1837.

Seven Cities of Delhi, Gordon Hearn. London; Thacker & Co., 1908.

Siege of Delhi, Handbook. Allahabad; Pioneer Press, 1907.

Storia do Mogor by Niccolao Manucci, translated by W. Irvine. London; John Murray, 1907.

Tavernier's Travels in India, edited by V. Ball. London; Macmillan & Co., 1889.

Tour in the upper provinces of Hindustan, by "A. D." London; Rivington, 1823.

Tours in Upper India, Archer. London; Bentley, 1833.

Travels in India, Von Orlich, translated by E. Lloyd. London; Brown, Green and Longmans, 1845.

Travels in the Mogul Empire by Francois Bernier, A. Constable. London; Constable & Co., 1901.

Two Native Narratives of the Mutiny in Delhi, translated by C. Metcalfe. London; A. Constable, 1898.

Āb-i-Ḥayāt, Muḥammad Ḥusain Āzād. Lahore, 1887.

Akbar Nāmah. Bibl. Ind.

'Ālamgīr Nāmah, Muḥammad Kāẓim. Bibl. Ind., 1868.

'Amal-i-Ṣāliḥ, Muḥammad Ṣāliḥ Lāhorī. MSS. in the Public Library, Lahore.

Āthāru-ṣ-Ṣanādīd, Sayyid Aḥmad Khān. Cawnpore and Lucknow editions.

Bādshāh Nāmah, 'Abdul Ḥamīd Lāhorī. Bibl. Ind., 1867—68.

Firishta. Lucknow, 1905.

Khazānah-i-'Āmirah, Ghulām 'Alī Bilgrāmī. Cawnpore, 1900.

Maāthir-i-'Ālamgīrī, Muḥammad Sāqī Musta'id Khān. Bibl. Ind., 1871.

Miftāḥu-t-Tawārīkh, *Beale*. Cawnpore, 1867.

Mirat-i-'Ālam. Bakhtāwar Khān. MSS. in possession of Maulvi Maḥmūdu-l-Ḥasan Khān of Tonk.

Mu'īnu-l-Āthār. Mu'īnu-d-Dīn, Agra.

Muntakhabu-l-Lubāb. Khāfī Khān, Bibl. Ind., 1869—74.

Siyaru-l-Mutaakhkhirīn. Ghulām Ḥusain. Lucknow.

Tārīkh-i-Jahān-Kushā-i-Nādirī. Mirzā Muḥammad Mahdī. Bombay.

Tārīkh-i-Muẓaffarī. Muḥammad 'Ali Khān Anṣārī. MSS. in Government Library, Allahabad.

Tuzak-i-Jahāngīrī. Aligarh, 1864.

Ẓafar Nāma-i-Shāhjahān, Muḥammad Dhukāullah. Delhi, 1897.

DELHI FORT.

A GUIDE

TO THE

HISTORICAL BUILDINGS AND GARDENS.

AFTER a reign of 11 years at Agra, Shāhjahān desired to remove his capital to Delhi, because, according to Bernier, "the excessive heat to which that city (Agra) is exposed during the summer rendered it unfit for the residence of a monarch". Other reasons for the move are said to have been "the broken ravines throughout the latter city, want of space in the Fort, narrowness of the streets, and the inconvenience caused to the inhabitants by the large crowds of troops and elephants and the retinues of the Emperor and his Umaras[1]; while Manucci[2] speaks of the healthiness of Delhi and of Shāhjahān's desire to perpetuate his memory by building a new capital there. After paying several visits to Delhi, he chose with the help of astrologers and *Hakims* a site on the mainland just south of Salimgarh, which had been founded in 1546 by Salīm Shāh, as a defence against the approach of Humāyūn. According to the contemporary historians, the foundation of the citadel was laid on the 12th Dhilḥijjah 1048 A. H. (1638 A. D.) and this date is corroborated by the inscriptions on the Khwābgāh. Shāh Nawāz Khān

[1] 'Amal-i-Sālih fol. 575—6.
[2] Storia do Mogor, Vol. I, p. 183.

gives 9th Muḥarram 1049[1] and Sayyid Aḥmad Khān, the author of *Āthāru-ṣ-Ṣanādīd*, states that among some old papers a horoscope of the Fort fell into his hands, and that in it the date of the foundation was recorded as Friday night, the 9th Muḥarram of the year 1049 A. H. (12th May, 1639 A. D.). The Fort, according to Shāh Nawāz Khān, author of the Maāthiru-l-Umarā, was constructed in 9 years, 3 months and a few days and completed in the 20th year of the Emperor's reign while he was at Kābul.

Makramat Khān, then the "Superintendent of Works," asked the Emperor to come and see it, and "on the 24th Rabī' II of 1058 A. H. (1648 A. D.)" Shāhjahān entered the Fort "through the gate facing the river" and held his first court in the Dīwān-i-'Āmm. The Emperor arrived at the Fort with a gorgeous retinue, Prince Dārā Shikoh scattering gold and silver over his father's head till he reached the gates[2]. The Palace buildings had already been decorated, and the courtyards covered with gorgeous carpets and hangings, while "deep red Kashmīr shawls covered each seat". "The buildings became the envy of the art galleries of China." The roofs, walls, and colonnades (*aiwāns*) of the Dīwān-i-'Āmm were hung with velvet, and silk from China and *khaṭā* (Chinese Turkestan) while a gorgeous canopy (*Aspak Dal bādal*), specially prepared for the occasion in the royal factory at Aḥmadābād,

[1] *Maāthiru-l-Umarā*, Persian Text, Vol. III, p. 464.

[2] A usual custom of Muhammadan Kings of India when entering the capital. Jahāngīr refers to a somewhat similar occasion in his Memoirs. *Tuzak-i-Jahāngīrī*, English translation by Rogers and Beveridge, p. 259.

and measuring 70 *gaz* by 45 *gaz* and costing a *lac* of rupees, was raised by "3,000 active *farrāshes*".

The canopy was supported by silver columns and surrounded by a silver railing. The hall of the Dīwān-i-'Āmm was enclosed on this occasion by a golden railing, while the throne was provided with a special canopy, fringed with pearls, and supported by golden pillars, wreathed with bands of studded gems. The Emperor still further signalised the occasion by the distribution of lavish gifts. The Begam Ṣāhiba received a *lac* of rupees, Prince Dārā, a special robe of honour, jewelled weapons, and an increase from the rank of ten to twenty thousand horse, a caparisoned elephant, and two *lacs* of rupees. The Princes Sulaimān Shikoh and Sipihr Shikoh received, respectively, daily allowances of Rs. 500 and Rs. 300 in addition to their original pay; the Prime Minister, S'adullah Khān, a robe of honour and a *nādrī* (a jewelled dagger) with the rank of 7,000 horse, Rāja Biṭṭhal Dās a robe and the rank of 5,000 foot and 4,000 horse.

Makramat Khān, under whose supervision the Fort and its buildings were completed, received the rank of *Panj Hazārī*.

The above is an abstract of Muḥammad Ṣālih's account of the inauguration ceremony, and the Palace is said to have been somewhat similarly decorated on the occasion of Aurangzeb's accession.

The Fort is an irregular octagon in plan with its two long sides on the east and west and the six smaller ones on the north and south. It measures about one mile and a half in circumference, the total length being some 3,000 feet and the breadth 1,800 feet. On the river front the walls are 60 feet in height, while on the land side they rise to 110 feet, of which 75 feet are above the level of the ground and the ditch. The latter is 75 feet wide and 30′ 0″ in depth. Faced with hewn stone and filled with water, it was, writes Bernier, formerly stocked with fish, and he says that in his opinion "a battery of moderate force would soon level the walls with the ground". "Adjoining the ditch are large gardens, full of flowers and green shrubs at all times, which, contrasted with the stupendous walls, produce a beautiful effect." These gardens were still to be seen in a neglected state before the Mutiny. Next to them was a big square where the royal horses were exercised and branded, and it was here that the tents of those Rājas were pitched who mounted guard in their weekly turn but would object to trust themselves within the walls of the Fort. "The Rājas," writes Bernier, "never mount within a fortress, but invariably without the walls, under their own tents not enduring the idea of being confined during four-and-twenty hours, and always refusing to enter any fortress unless well attended, and by men, determined to sacrifice their lives for their leaders". Hearn (Seven Cities of Delhi) says that to the south of this square a large tank of red sandstone, 500′×150′, connected with the canal in the C̲h̲āndnī C̲h̲auk and named after Lord Ellenborough, was built about 1846. The precincts of the tank were subsequently used by the mutineers as their cavalry camp in 1857.

The low ground to the east between the Fort and the river was used, Bernier adds, for elephant fights and "there the corps belonging to the *Omrahs* or lords, and those of the Rājas or gentile princes, pass in review before the Sovereign who witnesses the spectacle from the window of the palace ;" and he himself was once in danger, on this low ground, from an attack by an infuriated elephant. Manucci (*Storia do Mogor*), writing in much the same strain, says that "beneath the royal balconies there is, night and day, a mad elephant kept, for ostentation"

Other names associated with the building of the Fort besides that of Makramat Khān, already mentioned, are Ghairat Khān, Governor of Delhi [afterwards appointed as Governor of Thaṭha where he died in 1640 A. D. (1050 A. H.)] 'Izzat Khān, afterwards, Governor of Sindh, 'Ali Vardī Khān also appointed eventually to a Governorship, and two "master builders," if one may use the term, Ḥāmid (whose name is still commemorated by the Kūchā Ustā Ḥāmid near the Jāmi' Masjid) and Aḥmad. The Emperor is also said to have made certain modifications in the designs from time to time. Sayyid Aḥmad Khān no doubt owing to the presence of the portrait of Orpheus in the 'pietra dura' work in the Dīwān-i-'Āmm, has assumed that some Italian architect was also employed, but it would seem probable that the Italians were responsible for this particular branch of decoration only, the general arrangement and main details of the buildings being essentially eastern. The Fort is said to have cost 100 *lacs* of rupees of which half was spent on the walls and half on the buildings within.

Another historian, Bakhtāwar Khān, writing in the reign of Aurangzeb, also gives the cost of the various buildings as follows :—

	Lacs.
Fort and buildings within it	60
Royal mansions	28
Shāh Maḥal (Dīwān-i-Khāṣṣ), including silver ceiling and fittings	14
Imtiāz Maḥal (Rang Maḥal) with bed-chamber and surroundings	5½
Daulat Khāna-Khāṣṣ-o-'Āmm (Dīwān-i-'Āmm) .	2
Ḥayāt Bakhsh garden with the Ḥammām . .	6
The palace of the Begam Ṣāḥiba[1] and other royal ladies	7
Bāzārs, and squares for the Imperial workshops .	4
The Fort walls and moat	21

Workmen's wages amounted to ten million rupees.

Red sandstone and marble for the construction were provided by the governors and rājas of the localities where these materials were obtainable, and the former material was also brought down in large quantities from Fateḥpūr Sīkrī, by boat.

The Fort is known by many names. In the reigns of Shāhjahān and Aurangzeb it was styled *Qala'-i-Mubārak* (the Fortunate Citadel), or *Qala'-i-Shāhjahānābād*, and it is under this latter title that we find references to it in the historical works of the period. In the reign of Bahādur Shāh II, the last titular Emperor of Delhi, it was known as *Qala'-i-Mu'alla* (the Exalted Fort). This name occurs in the works of the Urdu poets of the time and accounts for the language of the Court being styled *Urdū-i-Mu'alla.*

[1] The title of Jahānārā Begam, eldest daughter of Shāhjahān.

It is recorded that in 1132 A. H. (1719 A. D.) much damage was done to the Fort and city by an earthquake lasting a month and two days (*Tārīkh-i-Muẓaffarī*). The buildings were also considerably damaged during the conflicts between the Marathas and Aḥmad Shāh Durānī in 1173 A. H. (1759 A. D.). Āzād Bilgrāmī, a contemporary writer, states "that Ibrāhīm Khān Kārdī, whom Bādu had brought in his company from the Deccan, had European artillery with him. He fired at the Fort with three guns from the *Retī* side (lit. "sandy place;" the sandy foreshore between the Fort and river is referred to) which lies below the Fort on the east, and discharged cannon balls like rain on the Asad Burj Muthamman Burj and other royal buildings, which resulted in great damage to the Dīwān-i-Khāṣṣ, Rang Maḥal, Motī Maḥal and Shāh Burj; but the Fort, on account of its great strength, remained undamaged"

It is a great pity that the lesser buildings and courts were removed after the Mutiny; for, without the courts and corridors connecting the buildings that are left to-day, the latter lose much of their meaning and beauty. The harem courts and gardens to the west of the Rang Maḥal, Mumtāz Maḥal, and the Khurd Jahān have all disappeared, together with a building known as the "Silver Palace" which stood some little distance to the west of the latter. The royal store-rooms, kitchens, and the Regalia chambers, which lay to the north of the court of the Dīwān-i-'Āmm have, together with the Mahtāb Bāgh and the western half of the Ḥayāt Bakhsh garden, given place to Military barracks and the parade ground. North again of the Ḥayāt Bakhsh garden, and between it and the north outer wall of the Fort, lay the houses, harems, and gardens of the Royal Princes. These have also disappeared. In the extreme north-west corner of the enclosure were the royal stables and stores, while the areas between the arcaded street, running due north from the Delhi gate to the north end of the Mahtāb Bāgh, and the west outer wall, were occupied by the houses of the enormous retinue attached to the Court.

The best known of these is the LAHORE GATE, situated in the centre of the west wall, and at the end of the principal thoroughfare of Delhi, the Chāndnī Chauk. The gate is of imposing design and contains three storeyed rooms. The entrance arch, 41 feet in height by 24 feet, is flanked by half octagon towers crowned by open octagonal pavilions, while between the latter is a screen of dwarf, coupled Chhatrīs, crowned by seven miniature domes of white marble, and terminated by tapering minarets, topped by lanterns. Above the entrance arch is a verandah crowned by a *Chhajja* (the sloping slab cornice seen on nearly every Indian building) but the arcade below it is now closed owing to the upper rooms of the gate having been adapted for use as officer's quarters. The 'flame shaped' battlements, which continue round the whole extent of the wall, are especially imposing.

The gate is additionally protected by a barbican, the work of Aurangzeb (1658-1707 A. D.). The walls of the latter are 40′ 0″ in height, the corners of the western wall being emphasised by pavilions. The entrance gate of the barbican is on the north side and measures 40′ 0″ in height by 24 feet in width, being surmounted by an embattled parapet, flanked by slender minarets. It is said that Shāhjahān, while in prison at Agra, wrote to his son Aurangzeb regarding these barbicans, saying "you have made the Fort a bride, and set a veil before her face". The original wooden draw-bridge of the barbican has gone, being replaced by bridges built by Akbar II (Mughal Emperor, 1806-1837). The inscription on the arch of the bridge states that these bridges (the second being at the Delhi gate), were built in his reign under the superintendence of "Dilāwaru-d-Daulah, Robert Macpherson, Bahādur, Diler Jang".

The DELHI GATE lies in the southern wall of the Fort and is so called as it faces the sites of the older cities. It is similar in design to the gate previously described, but is rendered more interesting by the presence of two stone elephants, standing at either side of the entrance arch. There are many theories put forward as to the history of the original elephants and their riders, and those that derive them originally from, Gwalior and Agra Fort have been proved to be without foundation. One of these theories is that their riders were the celebrated Rajpūt heroes Jaimal and Paṭṭa, but it seems more probable that the figures were only those of *mahāwats*, and that the animals were ordinary fighting elephants. The strict religious views of Aurangzeb would not tolerate the presence of the statues, and he ordered their demolition. Nothing more was heard of them till 1863, when, during the demolition of certain of the old buildings for military purposes, some 125 fragments of the original statues were found buried in the Fort. Three years later, an elephant was reconstructed from these fragments and set up in the Queen's gardens (opposite the Railway Station). In 1892 the statue was removed to a site in the Chāndnī Chauk and ten years later to another position in front of the Institute.

In 1903, at the instance of Lord Curzon, the present statues were erected, but the original fragments (now placed in the Museum) could not be re-used owing to the mutilation they had undergone. The work was entrusted to Mr. R. W. Mackenzie, an artist with experience of Indian Art, and the work was carried out from his models by Indian workmen. It is inconceivable how any doubt could ever have existed as to the original position of the statues. Bernier clearly places them at the Delhi gate, and his statement is backed up by that of de Thevenot, who saw them a few years later. The misconception seems to have arisen largely from the *Āthāru-ṣ-Ṣanādīd*, the later edition of which, published long after the author's death, places them at the Naubat Khāna. In the first edition they are placed before the Delhi gate. Carr Stephen (*Archæology of Delhi*, pp. 221-3) places them before the Naubat Khāna and Keene (*Guide to Delhi*, p. 18) before the Delhi gate, the former authority being of the opinion that Bernier's descriptions of the gates are so faulty that they are correct with respect to neither. Bernier, however, after describing the statues, clearly states that " after passing through the gate at which they stand there is a long and spacious street provided with a central canal," which is also referred to by M. de Thevenot. The only street of this kind in the Fort, as is proved by the old plans, was that running due north and south from the square in front of the Naubat Khāna. Bernier's description of the Lahore gate is rendered more explicit by his reference to the "roofed street (the *Chhatta Chauk*, see page 7), leading therefrom and bordered on either side by shops". It may be added that excavation, in connection with the erection of the present statues, disclosed further overwhelming evidence in the nature of the original foundations.

The Delhi gate is protected by a barbican, similar to that in front of the Lahore gate, the bridge being also erected in the reign of Akbar II, by Robert Macpherson[1].

There are three other gates to the Fort besides those two already mentioned. One leads into Salīmgaṛh, and through it the King-Emperor passed at the State Entry of the Coronation Darbār, 1911. Near it was formerly an old bridge built by Jahāngīr in 1031 A. H. (1621 A. D.), but this was removed to make way for the present railway bridge. The old bridge had five arches and was built of rubble, springing flush from the face of the abutments. It was strengthened by a series of arched ribs, springing from corbels projecting from the faces of the abutments, and giving it an appearance of lightness with great strength. The inscription from this bridge is now in the Museum. The present bridge, like the gate, is modern. There is also a postern or wicket gate (*khiṛkī*) between the

[1] Son of Andrew Macpherson, born in 1774 in the Parish of Thingupie, Invernesshire, entered the Honourable East India Company's service in 1794, became Lieutenant, 25th April 1797, Captain 27th February 1805, Major, 22nd January 1817, and died at Delhi, January 6th, 1823.

bridge and the Shāh Burj bastion. The *Khiẓrī*, or "Water gate" lies under the Muthamman Burj, and it was this gate which Captain Douglas desired might be thrown open, on the morning of the 11th May 1857, so that he might go down and reason with the mutineers, who had assembled on the low ground near the river.

Some few yards south of the Rang Maḥal is a wicket in the base of the wall, closed up, as it would seem from the character of the masonry, by the Mughals themselves. An attempt was made to excavate the ground at the back, but nothing was found, save what appeared to be a large underground drain. The story that it was known as the "King's gate," which was only used to take the dead body of the King out of the palace for burial, is an attractive one, but lacks confirmation. The "Water gate" outside the Asad Burj is of an extremely interesting and characteristic design, but owing to its position is but seldom visited. The inner gateway is reached by a long flight of steps and protected by a "barbican," with an outer gate facing the river.

THE CHHATTA CHAUK is the roofed street referred to by Bernier which leads from the Lahore gate to a point west of the Naubat Khāna and is described by Fergusson "as the noblest entrance known to any existing palace". It measures some 266 feet in length and 27 feet in width, with a central octagonal court open to the sky. On both sides of the roadway there are 32 arched cells, at first floor and ground floor levels. Muḥammad Ṣāliḥ, Shāhjahān's Court Chronicler, refers to this arcade as the *Bāzār-i-Musaqqaf* (covered *bāzār*).

The central portion, open to the sky, was styled the *Chhatta Manzil* (Vaulted Arcade), the historian adding, "that a building like this vaulted market had never been seen before by the peopel of India," and that it owed its conception to the Emperor, "who takes much interest in the construction of buildings". Bishop Heber in describing his visit to Akbar II refers thus to the *Chhatta Chauk*. "We were received with presented arms by the troops of the palace, drawn up within the barbican, and proceeded, still on our elephants, through the noblest gateway and vestibule I ever saw. It consists, not merely of a splendid Gothic arch in the centre of the great gate-tower—but, after that, of a long vaulted aisle, like that of a Gothic cathedral, with a small, open, octagonal court in the centre, all of granite[1], and all finely carved with inscriptions from the Qurān, and with flowers. This ended in a ruinous and exceedingly dirty stable-yard." The east end of this arcade opened on to a courtyard, some 200′ 0″ square, and surrounded by colonnades, used by the *Umarās* of the Emperor's guard. At the south-west corner of this square stood certain public buildings where the Emperor's *Nāẓir* (Superintendent of the household) contracted business. In its centre was a tank[2] fed by the canals which ran north and south towards the Mahtāb and Ḥayāt Bakhsh gardens and Delhi gate, respectively. On either side of the canals were the arcaded streets which have already been referred to on page 6. Bernier describes these streets

[1] The masonry is actually brick, externally plastered.

[2] The tank was filled after the Mutiny, but it was there that 49 Christians—men, women and children—were massacred by the Mutineers on May 16, 1857.

as being raised about 4½ feet from the ground and being about 4 feet wide, in front of a row of arched rooms—closed arcades—running the entire length of the street. It was here that the lesser officials used to transact business and the *Manṣabdārs* or inferior *Umarās* were wont to mount guard during the night. Once a week, in regular rotation, the guard duty was performed by them and, while on guard, they had their meals supplied by the King. In return according to Bernier, they had to make the *taslīm*[1], or salute of grateful acknowledgment of the royal gift, three times by turning the face towards the King's residence and raising the hand to the head and then lowering it to the ground.

At the east side of the square, and within a stone railing, stood the NAUBAT or NAQQĀRKHĀNA (the Royal Drum-House). The tank and square, with its surrounding buildings and the stone railings, have now all disappeared, but it is hoped to be able, eventually, to demarcate their former positions by lawns and shrubberies as has been done in the case of the gardens within the present archœological area.

This building measures some 99′ 0″ by 68′ 0″ and is 56′ 6″ high from the level of the plinth to the top of the roof. The gateway measures 29′ 0″ in height by 16′ 0″ in width. It must be remembered that the present plinth of this building is modern, the visitor being intended to enter at the level of the Dīwān-i-'Āmm court. The plinth is shortly to be removed, so that it will be

[1] 'On taking leave or presentation, or on receiving a *mansab*, or a *jāgīr*, or a robe of honour, or an elephant, or a horse, it is a rule to make three *taslīms*; but only one is performed on all other occasions (*i.e.*) when, salaries are paid or presents are made : cf, *Āīn-i-Akbarī*, Persian Text, Vol. I, pp. 74 and 156-7.

possible to enter at the original level. Buildings formerly existed at the north and south ends of the Naubat Khāna, but these were taken away after the Mutiny, their position being now indicated by shrubberies. "Five times a day the royal band used to play in this lofty hall; on Sundays the music was kept up the whole day because it was a day sacred to the sun, and the same honour was paid to the day of the week on which the King was born." Bernier, who was at first deafened by the noise, and found it unbearable, eventually grew accustomed to the royal music and discovered "grandeur, solemnity, and even melody in it" A "Naubat Khāna" is often found in royal palaces. The one at Fatḥpūr Sīkrī is well known, while they are often seen, and still used, in the residences of Indian chiefs. The building served as quarters for officers stationed in the Fort till 1907, when the modern additions were removed and the building restored as far as possible to its former appearance[1]. The two small rooms in the basement on either side of the entrance, now occupied by the Custodian, were used, till 1911, as the Museum of Archæology.

Passing through the entrance of the Naubat Khāna, the visitor reaches the court of the Dīwān-i-'Āmm (Hall of Public Audience). Through this entrance none could pass mounted except Princes of the Blood Royal; ambassadors, ministers and grandees of the highest dignity, alighted here and walked on foot. Even in the last days of a subsidised Mughal Emperor, the entrance was jealously guarded, and when Mr. Francis Hawkins, Resident at Delhi (a gentleman whose

[1] The upper storey is occupied by the Indian War Museum.

energy went beyond his discretion), was removed from his appointment, the most serious charge against him was that he had violated the sanctity of the royal palace, by riding under the gateway of the Naubat Khāna. The court, now reached, was originally 550′ 0″ in length by 300′ 0″ in width, and surrounded with arcaded apartments, which, says Bernier, "have no buildings over them". Each "bay" of the arcade was separated by a wall, "yet in such a manner that there is a small door to pass from one to the other". The rooms were deep, raised almost 3½ feet from the ground, and were occupied by the *Umarās* on duty. They were decorated on special occasions, and it is said that the *Umarās* vied with each other in the splendour of their adornment. These surrounding arcades were demolished after the Mutiny, but their former position has now been indicated by shrubberies. It should be remarked that the shrubbery on the south side of the court is, of necessity, placed further north than the original arcade, owing to the presence of the military road outside the railings to the south. Outside to the north of the courtyard stood the imperial kitchen (Keene, "*Guide to Delhi*," p. 125).

The great hall of the DĪWĀN-I-'ĀMM was the central feature of the eastern side of the court, while to the north of this building was a gate leading to the forecourt in front of the Dīwān-i-Khāṣṣ. In the days of the later Mughal Empire the appearance of the Dīwān-i-'Āmm was not improved by the addition, behind it, of the houses of the "Heir apparent," built in the bastard European style of architecture which was fashionable in India during that period. The building, which has lost its original covering of white shell plaster and gilding, stands, on a plinth some 4′ 0″ in height and measures 80′ 0″ long by 40′ 0″ in breadth; it is some 30′ 0″ high from the top of the plinth to the level of the roof parapet, the north-west and south-west angles of which are emphasised by dwarf pavilions. The building is open on the north, south and west, the outer walls being shaded by a deep *C͟hhajja.* Above the latter can still be seen traces of the old external decoration. The inside of the hall is divided up by columns into three aisles, each of nine compartments, each compartment being formed by four pillars some 16′ 0″ apart, which support engrailed arches ranging from the back wall to the façade of the building. The western façade is adorned with ten columns supporting engrailed arches. Set in a recess in the centre of the back wall is a marble "baldachino" known as the *Nas͟hīman-i-Ẓill-i-Ilāhī* (the seat of the shadow of God), panelled with marble and inlaid with precious stones. In front of this "baldachino" stands a four-legged marble dais, measuring some 7′ 0″×3′ 0″, said to have been used by the *Wazīr* when presenting petitions to the Emperor seated under the canopy above, with some of his sons at his right and left and the eunuchs standing behind flapping away flies with peacock's tails. A railed space, some 40′ 0″ in length by 30′ 0″ in width, was, according to Bernier reserved round the "baldachino" for the "whole body of the *Omrahs*, the *Rājas* and the Ambassadors all standing, their eyes bent downward, and their hands crossed". The remainder of the hall served as another reserved space for yet another rank of officials, while outside the Dīwān-i-'Āmm was the *Gulāl-Bāṛī* (red enclosure), reserved for minor officials, the general throng attending the *darbār* standing outside this last enclosure. When Bishop Heber saw it in 1824-1825, the hall, once richly "painted and covered with gold," "was full of lumber of all descriptions, broken palanquins and empty boxes, and the throne so covered with pigeon's dung, that its ornaments were scarcely discernible".

The *pietra dura* work of the recess behind the "baldachino" is worthy of special notice. The original work is said to have been executed by Austin de Bordeaux, a renegade European jeweller, and the designs represent flowers, fruit and birds in a most natural manner. Among the other designs the Frenchman introduced a picture of Orpheus playing on his lute, with a lion, a hare, and a leopard lying charmed at his feet. This tablet was removed after the capture of the Palace in 1857, and placed in the South Kensington Museum, while eleven others of the inlaid panels were also removed. They were restored to their original position some years ago at the instance of Lord Curzon. It was fortunate that old drawings of the mosaics existed, from which it was possible to restore the decoration to its original form, and for this purpose an Italian 'mosaicista' was brought specially to India and the work completed in 1909.

The following note taken from the Archæological Survey Annual for 1902-03, and written by Sir John Marshall, is of special interest in this connection :—

> "The decoration is more particularly famous for the panels of black marble, inlaid with a variety of coloured stones in designs of birds

and flowers. These panels are the sole examples in India of this particular form of technique. The most justly famous among them is one representing the figure of Orpheus sitting under a tree and fiddling to a circle of listening animals[1]. At the time of the Mutiny in 1857 a good many of these panels, which are quite small, were picked out and mutilated. Twelve of them including the representation of Orpheus as well as four larger and seven smaller panels, were appropriated by Captain (afterwards Sir John) Jones, and sold by him for £500 to the British Government, who deposited them in the South Kensington Museum.

"In 1882 all the inlay in the lower half of the back wall of the recess was restored under the supervision of Major H. H. Cole, the then Curator of Monuments in India. The work was executed with great care, but unhappily some of the stones employed in the new work matched badly with the originals. The difference between them is particularly noticeable in the background of the panels; a greyish black Indian marble having been used to replace the intensely black and finely grained marble, only procurable in Italy. In some other respects also the new work is inferior, the designs being harsher and the

[1] A beautiful chromo-lithograph of this is published by Major H. H. Cole in his report on Delhi in the series entitled the "Preservation of National Monuments in India". He also gives a general view of the back of the throne.

technique coarser. The upper portion of the wall was not repaired by Major Cole, because he hoped that the panels in England might be recovered at some future time and it appeared inexcusable to resort to artificial renovation so long as the originals were known to exist elsewhere. During the past year (1902) a strong appeal for the recovery of these panels was made by the Government of India, and the trustees of Victoria and Albert Museum were kind enough to agree to their return.

"It had been hoped that the plaques would reach India in time to be restored for the ceremonies of the Investiture of the two Indian Orders held in connection with the Delhi Darbar (Lord Curzon's Darbar of 1903) and the occasion would indeed have been an appropriate one of which to emblemise, by the restoration of the mosaics, the generous policy which the Government have now adopted towards the relics of antiquity, as opposed to the proverbial vandalism of earlier days. Unfortunately the plaques did not arrive till the last days of December, and their restitution had to be deferred until after the Darbar. They have now been replaced behind the throne; and many other panels, also in the upper portion of the walls, have been cleaned of the lac with which they were covered, and their mutilated surfaces repolished. There still, however, remain some of the gaps where panels are partly or wholly missing, and these will be gradually filled up, as opportunity offers, in accordance with the ancient designs. But it will take some time before the precise stones used can be identified and procured from Europe, and it will very probably be found necessary to get the panels executed in Florence or to obtain artists from Italy to do the work in India.

"Something remains to be said concerning the date and style of these plaques. Tradition has it that the decoration of the throne was the workmanship of Austin de Bordeaux, the celebrated French artificer, who is said to have been employed by the Emperor Shāhjahān, both on the palace at Delhi and on the Taj at Agra. The figure of Orpheus, indeed, is pointed out by the native guides as a portrait of Austin de Bordeaux himself. The story seems apocryphal. Perhaps it was suggested by the obviously Italian character of the panel designs; but it should be observed that the black marble of their backgrounds and the majority of the inlaid stones are of Italian, and not Indian provenance and it is not unreasonable to suppose, therefore, that they were not only designed but actually executed in an Italian studio and afterwards imported into this country.

"The arabesques, on the other hand, which decorate the interspaces between the panels, are of pure Indian style and Indian workmanship without a vestige of foreign influence. Mr. Havell, referring to the decoration of the Delhi Throne, in a recent article in *The Nineteenth Century and After*, has suggested that it has been wrongly attributed to Shāhjahān's reign and ought rather to be inferred to the early part of the eighteenth century. He rightly insists on its inferiority in point of style to that of the Taj at Agra, and further argues that the naturalistic representations of birds and animals, had they existed in the time of Aurangzeb, would scarcely have been left unmutilated by that iconoclast Emperor. The latter argument is not convincing, since parallel instances may be cited of other figures which must often have been seen by Aurangzeb, yet managed to escape violation at his hands. Nor ought mere inferiority of style to be pressed too far as evidence of date. The *pietra dura* of Shāhjahān's reign in the Lahore Fort is equally inferior to that of the Taj, and in the case of the Delhi Throne the task of the artists was a peculiarly difficult one. The basis of this decoration was a number of square and oblong panels of varying sizes and of wholly unfamiliar styles. There are few artists who could create an harmonious design out of such material, and least of all a Mughal artist, tied down by the strictest traditions of form and colour, both alike unsuitable to the task he had to perform. With such limitations it is not surprising that the result appears grotesque, or that the arabesques, which serve to combine the panels into a general scheme of decoration, compared unfavourably in style with those of the Taj."

The European traveller Bernier (*Travels in the Mogul Empire*, pp. 261-3) has left an excellent account of the ceremonials for which the Dīwān-i-'Āmm was used.

"During the hour and a half, or two hours, that this ceremony (the *darbār*) continues, a certain number of the royal horses pass before the throne, that the King may see whether they are well used and in a proper condition. The elephants come next, their filthy hides having been well washed and painted as black as ink, with two large red streaks from the top of the head down to the trunk, where they meet. The elephants are covered with embroidered cloth; a couple of silver bells are suspended to the two ends of a massive silver chain placed over their back, and white cow tails[1] from Great Tibet, of large value, hang from the ears like immense whiskers. Two small elephants, superbly caparisoned, walk close to the colossal creatures, like slaves appointed to their service. As if proud of his gorgeous attire and of the magnificence that surrounds him, every elephant moves with a solemn and dignified step; and when in front of the throne, the driver, who is seated on his shoulder, pricks

[1] The tails of the Tibetan ox or yak, called chowries, still in common use in India.

him with a pointed iron, animates him and speaks to him, until the animal bends on one knee, lifts his trunk on high and roars aloud, which the people consider as the elephant's mode of performing the *taslīm* or usual reverence.

"Other animals are next introduced; tame antelopes kept for the purpose of fighting with each other;[1] *Nilgaux,*[2] or grey oxen, that appear to me to be a species of elk; rhinoceroses; large *Bengale* buffaloes with prodigious horns which enable them to contend against lions and tigers; tame leopards, or panthers, employed in hunting antelopes; some of the fine sporting dogs from Usbec, of every kind, and each dog with a small red covering; lastly every species of the birds of prey used in the field sports for catching partridges, cranes, hares, and even, it is said, for hunting antelopes, on which they pounce with violence, beating their heads and blinding them with their wings and claws."[3]

"Besides this procession of animals, the cavalry of one or two of the *Omrahs* (*Umarās*) frequently pass in review before the King; the horsemen

[1] The Emperor Akbar was very fond of this sport, and in the *Āīn-i-Akbarī* (pp. 218-222) will be found full details regarding the kinds of fighting deer, how they fought, together with elaborate regulations as to the betting allowed on such encounters.

[2] Literally "blue cows," the Hindustānī name being Nīlgāo.

[3] See the illustration of a Barkūt eagle attacking a deer, from Atkinson's 'Siberia' at p. 385, Vol. I, of Yule's *Marco Polo*, second ed., 1875, and the Chapter (XVIII, same vol.) on the animals and birds kept by the Kaan for the chase.

being better dressed than usual, the horses furnished with iron armour, and decorated with an endless variety of fantastic trappings.

"The King takes pleasure also in having the blades of cut-lasses tried on dead sheep, brought before him without the entrails and neatly bound up. Young *Omrahs*, *Mansebdars*, and *Gourze-berdars*[1] or mace-bearers, exercise their skill and put forth all their strength to cut through the four feet, which are fastened together, and the body of the sheep at one blow.

"But all these things are so many interludes to more serious matters. The King not only reviews his cavalry with particular attention, but there is not, since the war has been ended, a single trooper or other soldier whom he has not inspected, and made himself personally acquainted with, increasing or reducing the pay of some and dismissing others from the service. All the petitions held up in the crowd assembled in the *Am-Kas* (the Dīwān-i-'Āmm) are brought to the King and read in his hearing; and the persons concerned being ordered to approach are examined by the Monarch himself, who often redresses on the spot the wrongs of the aggrieved party."

The verandah on the first floor level at the back of the Dīwān-i-'Āmm and overlooking the garden in front

[1] *Gurz-bardār*, from *gurz*, a Persian word, signifying a mace or war-club.

of the Rang Maḥal is said to have been covered with shell-plaster, "polished like the brightness of the morning."

As has been previously mentioned, a gateway lay to the north of the Dīwān-i-'Āmm, leading to the first of the twin courtyards in front of the Dīwān-i-Khāṣṣ, now no longer in existence, but demarcated, like the other court immediately in front of that building, by shrubberies and lawns. In the middle of the western wall of this 'first courtyard' was a gate which gave entrance to the court of the Dīwān-i-Khāṣṣ, the Hall of Special Audience. A red cloth awning was stretched in front of this gateway and gave it the name of *Lāl Pardah* (red screen).

The buildings on the East wall of the Fort in the enclosed area.

The MUMTĀZ MAḤAL, now the Museum, is the southernmost of these buildings. Formerly one of the apartments of the Royal princesses, it has served as a Military prison (carvings by the prisoners can be still seen on the marble dadoes) and was also used, till recently, as the Sergeants' Mess, and for this purpose its original appearance had been completely changed. Old drawings and photos of the Fort, dating prior to the Mutiny, show it to have been a structure not unlike the neighbouring Rang Maḥal, covered with white shell plaster, and with the angles of its roof emphasised by dwarf pavilions, the external walls being shaded by a deep *Chhajja*. The latter has been reconstructed and, within, some of the original "glass" decoration has been exposed. It will be noticed that the plinth of the building is still buried, but this is shortly to be removed and the neighbouring ground laid out to the same level as the lawns to the north. Excavations made in 1911 revealed the remains of a small marble fountain basin in front of the building on the west side. It was also known as the 'Chhoṭā Rang Maḥal' or 'Khāṣṣ Maḥal' and it seems not unlikely that the water channel, which runs through the centre of the other buildings to the north, continued past it also. That the space between the Mumtāz Maḥal and the Rang Maḥal was filled with buildings in the days of the last Emperor of Delhi is evident from old photographs taken before the Mutiny, while it is probable that in the days of Shāhjahān, another smaller pavilion existed here[1], the range of arcades, which formed the south boundary of the garden of the Rang Maḥal, probably continuing through to the front of the east wall of the Fort; any interspaces between the buildings on the east outer wall would be filled with marble screens to prevent the inmates of the harem being seen from the low ground between the Fort and the river.

"Last of all the Seraglio buildings on the river face (*i.e.*, between the Mumtāz Maḥal and the Asad Burj) there came the Khurd Jahān (Little World). Why it was so called we do not know, unless within it there

[1] Hearn, *Seven Cities of Delhi*, states that a small pavilion known as the Small Sitting Place (*Chhoṭi Baiṭhak*), and a modern building the *Daryā* (River) *Maḥal* occupied this space. The latter building, he says, was more ornate than the others, and had a pediment on the river face surmounted by the figure of a bird. An old photograph of the Fort taken before the Mutiny shows a building of this design.

were collected different flowers and trees and all that was necessary to make it like the world on a small scale."[1]

The RANG MAḤAL (Palace of Colour), so called from the coloured decoration with which it was formerly adorned, lies immediately to the north of the Mumtāz Maḥal. The building was the largest of the apartments of the Royal Seraglio, and in the time of S͟hāhjahān was known as the Imtiyāz Maḥal (Palace of Distinction). The Court Chronicler writes of it that, "in excellence and glory it surpasses the eight-sided throne of heaven, and in lustre and colour it is far superior to the palaces in the promised paradise." It is indeed to be regretted that so few traces remain of its former elaborate decoration. The building measures externally 153′ 6″ by 59′ 3″, and, within, engrailed arches on twelve-sided piers divide the main apartment into fifteen bays, each 20′ 0″ square. These are cased in marble for 11′ 0″ of their height, the point at which the arches spring from plaster capitals. On the soffits of the outer row of arches can still be seen remains of the old gilded decoration in the form of conventional flowers. It is said that the original ceiling was of silver, but that in the reign of Farruk͟hsiyar it was taken off "to supply a pressing need," and replaced by one of copper. In the reign of Akbar II this latter was also removed and a wooden one put up. Muḥammad Ṣāliḥ writing in the reign of S͟hāhjahān, describes the original ceiling as being "gilded and ornamented with golden flowers." The eastern wall is pierced by five windows overlooking the river, and from there the ladies of the *zanāna* could

[1] *Op. cit.*, p. 161.

catch a glimpse of the elephant fights which took place on the sandy foreshore at the foot of the walls, and of which the Emperor was an interested spectator in the adjoining Muthamman Burj. Four of these windows are now filled with rectilinear tracery of a type reminiscent of Chinese decoration. The original glazing, which has entirely disappeared, was probably of panes of glass of that vivid colour still seen in one of the windows of the Ḥammām. The central window opening is enclosed by a frame of flamboyant swirls, bulbous domes, and surmounted by an umbrella shaped finial, the whole an unpleasant foretaste of the decadence which set in with the reign of Aurangzeb. At each end of the main hall are smaller chambers, surrounded by a marble dado, waist-high, the upper portions of the walls being relieved by conventional floral designs in plaster, set off with " glass " borders. Down the centre of the building runs a marble water channel with a central fountain basin, buried, till 1908, under a modern stone floor. 'Alī Mardān's canal, tapping the Jumna some six miles above Delhi to obtain the necessary fall, fed the Palace with many streams of limpid water which filled the tanks, played the fountains and poured " like a quick fall of stars " before the illuminated candle niches. But of all these waterways the most favoured was the Nahr-i-Bihisht (Stream of Paradise) so called by Shāhjahān himself.[1] Falling in a rippling cascade down the marble chute in the Shāh

[1] Manucci, *Storia do Mogor*, Irvine's translation, Vol. I, p. 184, says " Shāhjahān ordered some beautiful fish to be thrown into the canal with gold rings in their heads, each ring having one ruby and two seed-pearls."

Burj pavilion and flowing along the terrace that bordered the Ḥayāt Bakhsh garden, it traversed the chain of stately edifices that lined the eastern wall of the Palace—Ḥammām, Dīwān-i-Khāṣṣ and Khwābgāh—silently gliding beneath the Mīzān-i-'Adl, (" Scales of justice ") across a sun-bathed court into the cool of the Rang Maḥal. Thence, still southward, it passed through the little Rang Maḥal, Mumtāz Maḥal, and other buildings of the Imperial *zanāna*, sending out shoots to feed the many channels and fountains. As Bernier (*Travels in the Mogul Empire*, p. 267) tells us, " nearly every chamber has its reservoir of running water at its door ; on every side are gardens, delightful alleys, shady retreats, streams, fountains, grottoes, deep excavations that afford shelter from the sun by day, lofty divans and terraces, on which to sleep cool at night." Elsewhere he says, " The water of the canal......into the Seraglio, divides and intersects every part and falls into the ditches of the fortification."[1] Still despite the spoliation of its jewels and the lack of dancing waters, this fountain basin is by far the most charming of all those in the Fort, and is perhaps only surpassed in elegance by the fountain in the Muthamman Burj pavilion at Agra. Sayyid Ahmad says of the Rang Maḥal, " it has a tank, the beauty of which baffles description. It is made of marble and fashioned in such a way that it resembles a full blown flower. Its inlay of flowers and foliage in various coloured stones has been so finely executed that it is beyond the power of anyone to describe it. Although the tank is seven *gaz* square

[1] *Archæological Survey of India Annual Report*, 1907-1908, pp. 23-30.

yet it is of very little depth. It is just like the palm of a hand. The particular beauty of this is that, when it is full of rippling water, the foliage of the inlay work appears to wave to and fro. In its centre is a beautiful flower like a cup of marble ; moreover, on each curving point and arched cusp, flowers and leaves of coloured stones spring from creeping plants, and creeping plants from flowers and leaves. Within the cup you will find a hole through which the water bubbles up from a hidden channel underneath. The sheet of water falling from the edges of the cup and the waving of the plants and flowers under the dancing water are nothing less than a scene of magic."

Muḥammad Ṣāliḥ is likewise moved to enthusiasm : "In the midst of the Central Hall is a shallow tank designed on geometrical principles. It is decorated with points and on each point there is a hole through which the water of life bubbles out from the jets fixed above, enhancing the pleasantness of the surroundings and the beauty of the building. The mind of man, on perceiving this wonder, is amazed. The channels on the four sides, fed from this sunlike fountain, pour their waters in the form of a cascade, into a basin made of one piece of marble, and on leaving this the water flows into the main channel running into the midst (of the gardens). The stone of this basin is one of the wonders of the world and came from the Makrāna Quarry. By order of His Majesty, the basin was made square, four *gaz* by four *gaz*[1] with a depth of one and a half *gaz*. It was brought by means of a hundred

[1] These dimensions give the size as 10′ 5″ square × 4′ 0″ deep. Actual size is 10′ 3″ square × 3′ 10″ deep.

mechanical contrivances from Makrāna to Shājahānābād, a distance of one hundred *kuroh*,[1] and placed here."

The basin, to which the historian refers, stood for a long time in the Queen's Gardens, but was brought back in 1911 to the palace gardens and now stands in the centre of the large tank between the Rang Maḥal and the Dīwān-i-'Āmm. The courtyard, of which this large tank was the central feature, was formerly " so extensive that it was laid out as a garden with channels dotted with jets." Bishop Heber writing in the early years of the 19th century says that, " all these were destroyed when he saw the Fort and that instead wretched houses had been built." " The gardens contained an orchard 107 *gaz*×115 *gaz*,[2] which was surrounded by a screen-like railing of redstone. The railing was decorated with two thousand finials of gold. On the three sides of the courtyard beautiful houses and charming arcades were built seventeen *gaz* wide, and below the plinth of the palace, on the west side, lay this garden." The bottom of the large central tank, which measures 126′ 0″×123′ 6″, is now grassed, owing to the impossibility of allowing water to stand there, and so encouraging the breeding of mosquitoes.

The foundations of the houses and arcades, on the north and south sides of the garden, were located by excavation and are now represented by shrubberies, as is the colonnade on the third or west side, a continuation

[1] *Kuroh*=about 2½ miles. Distance as the crow flies between Makrāna and Delhi is about 186 miles.

[2] The measurement of the *gaz* varies considerably. It is between 2′ 8″ and 3′ 0″. It consists of two *hāths*, the *hāth* being the distance between the point of the elbow, when bent, and the tips of the fingers.

of the projecting block at the back of the Dīwān-i-'Āmm, and through which the Emperor passed from his private apartments to the Hall of Justice. " From the back of the King's private entrance to the *jharokha*[1] there is an open gallery overlooking the garden ; and thence a winding stairway leads direct to the colonnade below. It is easy to imagine the Emperor, wearied with the ministration of justice or bored by an audience of foreign embassies, seeking relief in the cool of the Rang Maḥal, resplendent with colour and marble, and musical with the subdued murmur of falling waters, and the voices of his chosen ladies." Sayyid Aḥmad states that, " near the corners of the Rang Maḥal were four stone kiosks which could be closed with *taṭṭīs* in the summer-time, and turned into *Khas*[2] *Khāna.*"

" It is fortunate that the historian has added a drawing[3] of the façade from which we are able to learn what these kiosks were like, for no vestige of them now remains except their foundations. They were by no means an improvement to the façade with their pointed roofs and slender shafts. The drawing—more accurate than the description—shows but two of these pavilions at the ends of the main façade. The accuracy of Sayyid Aḥmad's description may also be doubted on other points ; for it appears that there was never any marble above the necking of the piers and what he mistook for inlay was painted ornament."

" From this illustration we also learn that the arches of the façade were filled in with an open *pardah* screen,

[1] Lit. Showing place.
[2] A kind of coarse grass of which *taṭṭīs* are made.
[3] The original drawing may be seen in the Museum (Catalogue Ed. 1926, J. 21).

apparently of marble, the traces of which are still to be seen; while the centre opening was further elaborated by the introduction of moulded columns and a triple arch. Above the small screens were small windows filled with *jālī*, similar to that seen on the north and south façades. Altogether, the illustration makes the west front of the Maḥal more attractive than it is now under its coat of whitewashed plaster."[1] Carr Stephen and Keene both erroneously describe it as being built of "grey sandstone."

"From the Rang Maḥal the Emperor passed across a narrow court to his private apartments under the arcade before the Scales of Justice. This façade is of white marble and now shows no signs of having been coloured, all traces having been bleached out by the blaze of sun which beats fiercely on this wall throughout the day. Until recently there was a buttress wall jutting out some 3′ 0″ into the court at the west angle. A careful inspection showed that neither this wall nor the one on a corresponding position on the north side of the Khāṣṣ Maḥal[2] was structurally necessary, and as they were of obviously modern construction, the core being of modern bricks, they were demolished. It was then discovered that considerable traces of colour remained high up the wall where the protecting *Chhajja* had cast its shadow. From this it is safe to presume that the elaborate painted decoration of the interior originally extended to the exterior of the building, and I believe this instance to be unique."[3]

[1] *Op. cit.*
[2] Another name for the collection of rooms known as the Tasbīḥ Khāna, Khwābgāh, and Baiṭhak.
[3] *Op. cit.*

The following account of these buildings has been taken from Carr Stephen's *Archæology of Delhi*:— "Corresponding to the Royal Baths, and on the south of the Dīwān-i-Khāṣṣ, is a suite of rooms built throughout of marble and divided into two equal parts by the marble canal already described. Between these rooms and the Dīwān-i-Khāṣṣ the pavement is of marble and is about 46 feet wide."

"The Tasbīḥ Khāna (place where the praises of God are recounted by the telling of beads), Khwābgāh (dormitory) and Baiṭhak (place where people meet to sit and converse) form one building; the former consists of a row of three rooms facing the Dīwān-i-Khāṣṣ; a second row of three rooms behind this is known as the Khwābgāh, and the adjoining hall, which is about half the width of the Khwābgāh, was indiscriminately called the Baiṭhak or the Tosha Khānah (Ward Robe). The three apartments together may be equal in size to the Dīwān-i-Khāṣṣ." At the suggestion of the Hon. Mr. W. M. Hailey, the then Chief Commissioner of Delhi, two of the western apartments have been furnished in the Mughal manner, so that visitors to the Palace may be able to repicture the interior arrangements of a room during this period. "There is nothing particular to notice either in the Tasbīḥ Khāna or the Baiṭhak; the Khwābgāh, however, deserves more than passing attention. As already stated, it is the name of the three rooms in the centre of the building; the middle room is about 45 feet by 18 feet, those on its east and on its west are about half its size. The three rooms communicate with one another through arched doors in the centre room ; the walls were at one time inlaid with precious-stones which were pillaged by the attendants of the court, and have recently been repaired with great success. (Mr. Carr Stephen wrote his book in 1876.) In the northern and southern walls of the centre room there are arched doors covered with marble screens, and under the arches there are inscriptions of historical fame—the work of Sa'dullah Khān, the Wazīr of Shāhjahān. On the outer eastern face of the door of this room there is another inscription, which is also said to be the work of the same author."

English translation of the inscription on the southern and northern arches :—" Praise be to God ! how beautiful are these painted mansions and how charming are these residences : a part of the high heaven. When I say the high-minded angels are desirous of looking at them, if people from different parts and directions (of the world) should come (here) to walk round them as (they walk) round the old house (*Ka'ba*), it would be right ; and if the beholders of the two worlds should run to kiss their highly glorious threshold as (they kiss) the black stone (of *Ka'ba*), it would be proper. The commencement of this great fort, which is higher than the palace of the heavens and is the envy of the wall of Alexander ; and of these pleasant edifices and of the garden of Hayāt Bakhsh, which is to these buildings as the soul is to the body, and the lamp to an assembly ; and of the pure canal, the limpid water of which is to the person possessing sight as a world-reflecting mirror, and to the wise the unveiler of the secret world ; and of the water-falls, each of which you may say is the whiteness of the dawn or a tablet of secrets of the Table and the Pen (of Fate); and of the playing fountains, each of which is a hand of light rising to greet the inhabitants of heaven; or they are bright pearls alighting to reward the inhabitants of the earth; and of the tanks, full of the water of life (and) in its purity the envy of the light and the sun; announced on the 12th Dhilḥijjah in the 12th holy year of the ascension, corresponding to 1048 A.H., the delightful tidings of happiness to the people of the world. And the completion of it, which was effected at the expense of 50 *lacs* of rupees, on the 24th Rabī'u-l-Awwal in the 21st year of the auspicious ascension corresponding to 1058 A.H., by the glory of the happy feet of the sovereign of the earth, the lord of the world, the founder of these heavenly, pleasant mansions, Shihābu-d-Dīn Muhammad, the second Lord of felicity, Shāhjahān, the king champion of faith, opened the door of favour to the people of the world."

English translation of the verses on the wall[1]:

"May the Emperor of the world, Shāhjahān, by his good fortune, the second Lord of felicity,
In the royal palace, with great magnificence, ever be like the sun in the sky.
As long as foundation is indispensable with this building,
May the palace of his good fortune touch the highest heaven.
Wonderfully charming is this adorned palace:
A paradise embellished with a hundred beauties.

[1] The inscription has become obliterated and is now no longer traceable.

Dignity is a sign to represent its greatness ;
Felicity is in the embraces of its hall.
(Incomplete.)
(Incomplete.)
Whoever rubbed his head sincerely against its foot,
His honour increased, like (the swelling) of the (river) Jun (Jumna).
When time erected its wall,
It set a mirror before the face of the sun.
The face of its wall is so decorated, that it demands from the painters of
China a fee for showing its face.
Time extended such an (affectionate) hand over its head,
That the sky borrowed height from it.
In its playing fountains, and river-like tank,
The sky washed its face with the water of the earth.
As it is the seat of a just King,
So it is the King of all other buildings."

Count Von Orlich, visiting Delhi in 1843, says that " before the entrance to the residence of the Great Mogul, a pair of scales are suspended over a stone seat, to indicate that justice alone is administered in these apartments. As we entered the halls which lead to the King's apartments we saw a rhapsodist, who was sitting before the bed chamber of the Great Mogul and relating tales in a loud voice. A simple curtain was hung between him and the King, who was lying on a couch and whom these tales were to lull to sleep." (*Travels in India, Von Orlich*, Vol. II, p. 25.)

Adjoining the eastern wall of the Khwābgāh, and overlooking the river, is the domed balcony (also known as the *Burj-i-Ṭilā* or Golden Tower) which Bernier, who, however, had never seen it, praised so extravagantly. It is octagonal in plan and roofed by a dome, once cased in gilded copper and now covered with lime plaster. Three out of the eight sides of this room are cut off by the Khwābgāh, and of the remaining five sides which overlook the river, four are filled with marble screens ; in front of the fifth, which is in the middle of the Burj, there is a small covered balcony added by Akbar II, who also engraved an inscription on its arches and another on the western doorway of the Muthamman Burj.

English translation of the first inscription :

"Praise and thankfulness are worthy of the Lord of the world.
Who made such an Emperor the King of the age ;
Who is descended from a royal father and grandfather down from Tīmūr ;
(And is the) protector of the world, having his court (as high as the) sky, and soldiers (as numerous as) stars,
Mu'ī-nu-Dīn Abu-n-Naṣr Akbar, Ghāzī,
King of the world, conqueror of the age, and shadow of God,
On the face of Muthamman Burj, built anew such a seat that the sun and the moon sewed (fixed) their eyes on it.
Sayyidu-sh-Shu'arā was ordered to record its date,
So that the black letters may endure on the white (ground).

The Sayyid wrote the chronogram of this building :
'May the seat of Akbar S͟hāh be of exalted foundation. The year 1223.' "

English translation of the second inscription :

"O (thou who hath) fetters on thy legs, and a padlock on thy heart, beware !
And O (thou) whose eyelids are sewn up, and whose feet are deep in the mire, beware !
Thou art bound towards the west ; but thou hast turned thy face to the east.
O traveller ! Thou has turned thy back on thy destination, beware ! "

"The eunuchs," says Bernier, writing of the Mut͟hamman Burj, "speak with extravagant praise of a small tower, facing the river, which is covered with plates of gold in the same manner as the towers of Agra ; and its azure apartments are decorated with gold and azure, exquisite paintings and magnificent mirrors."

A projecting *burj* of this type on the east wall was a common feature of the Mug͟hal palacc and is found at Agra and Lahore. From it the Emperor used to appear to the throngs gathered below the Fort, while at Agra Jahāngīr caused a rope of bells to be suspended between the *burj* and the ground below, for the use of suppliants.

The *dars͟han* or 'showing' ceremony was considered a most important procedure and was observed daily by the earlier Mug͟hal Emperors. In a court where an Emperor's life was in hourly danger such a ceremony was the only sign by which his subjects knew whether he was alive. We read of one Emperor being even carried to the *jharokha* on his sick bed rather than omit the observance of the *darshan*. It is interesting to note that the ceremony was revived at the Coronation Darbar, Their Imperial Majestics King George V and Queen Mary appearing from the balcony of the Muthamman Burj to the crowd gathered on the ground between the Fort and the river.

The *Khizrī* gate below it has already been commented upon.

The original dome of the Muthamman Burj was of quite different section from the present one and was, as stated above, covered with copper. It was removed after the Mutiny, together with the copper coverings of the pavilions at the corners of the roof of the Dīwān-i-Khāṣṣ, and sold by the Prize Agent.

The DĪWĀN-I-KHĀṢṢ was also known as the Shāh Maḥal (Royal Palace). It, like the Dīwan-i-'Āmm, had a courtyard in front of it to the west, enclosed by colonnades. The entrance to the courtyard nearest the Dīwān-i-Khāṣṣ and known as the *Jilau Khāna* was on the west, and was kept screened by a red curtain, the *Lāl Pardah*. In this court the *Umarās* and nobles of highest rank were wont to wait on the Emperor. It was removed, together with the lesser court, which lay immediately to the west, after the Mutiny, but from old plans and ample evidence forth coming in the excavations, it has been possible to lay out the present lawns and shrubberies so as to demarcate with accuracy their former alignment.

The hall is 90′ 0″ in length and 67′ 0″ in width, and stands on a plinth 4′ 6″ in height. Fergusson considers it "if not the most beautiful, certainly the most highly ornamented of all Shāhjahān's buildings." The central chamber measures 48′ 0″ by 27′ 0″. The ceiling is flat and supported by engrailed arches. 'Pietra dura' work is freely used on the lower portions of the arch piers, the upper portions being treated with gilding and painting. A marble water channel, the same Nahr-i-Bihisht, 12′ 0″ in width, runs through the centre of the hall. The marble daïs is said to have supported the famous peacock throne of Shāhjahān, valued at £12,037,500,[1] which was removed by Nādir Shāh in 1739. Over the arches at the north and south ends of the central chamber will be noticed the famous inscription : "If there is a paradise on the face of the earth, it is this, it is this, it is this."

This building is perhaps bound up more closely than any other with the history of the Mughal Empire. The favourite resort of the Emperor who built it, it witnessed in turn the heyday and the decline of the house of Tīmūr.

"Here, in 1716, the Scottish Surgeon, Gabriel Hamilton, who cured the Emperor Farokhsīr, on the eve of his marriage, was rewarded by the permission for his employers to establish a factory, and to maintain a territory of 38 towns on the banks of the Hūghli, which was the foundation of the 'Presidency of Fort William,' and all that has since sprung therefrom."[2]

[1] Tavernier's Travels, Vol. I, pp. 384-85. Bernier gives 4 Karors of rupees or 60 million French *livers*. But Tavernier's valuation is probably correct since he estimates its cost at 160,500,000 *livers* which when worked out yields £12,037,500, the value of a *liver* being equal to 1*s*. 6*d*.

[2] Keene, *Handbook to Delhi*, p. 134. The author adds, "Dr. Busteed, in 'Echoes of Old Calcutta,' discredits this and endeavours to show that the story has very little, if any, foundation in fact ;" though it should be mentioned that this incident of the granting of a "Royall Phirmaund" has been accepted as authentic by Beckles Wilson in *Ledger and Sword* (Vol. II, pp. 59-61).

In it Nādir Shāh received the submission of Muḥammad Shāh (Mughal Emperor 1719-1748) in 1739, and deprived him of the most valuable treasures of his ancestors. The predatory hordes of Jāṭs, Marāṭhas and Rohillas, which harassed in turn the last Emperors of the line, despoiled it of its remaining treasures, while it is said to have been the place wherein the aged Shāh 'Ālam was blinded by the brigand Ghulām Qādir. In it Lord Lake was thanked for delivering the tottering empire from the house of Scindhia, while in May 1857 the mutineers chose it as the edifice wherein to proclaim Bahādur Shāh II once more Emperor of Hindustān, all unwitting that some seven months later he was to be tried in the same hall for his life.

In earlier times it was known as the Shāh Maḥal or Daulat Khāna-i-Khāṣṣ and even, by a misnomer, as the *Ghusl Khāna.*[1] 'Abdul Ḥamīd Lāhorī, Shāhjahān's

[1] Manucci refers to the Dīwān-i-Khāṣṣ as the *Ghusl-Khāna* in the following passage :

> " Four horses, ready saddled for emergency, are kept near the door of the Ghusl Khāna, the place where audience is given and justice dispensed." Elsewhere, " This prince (Shāh 'Ālam) held me in such affection that he granted me permission to enter the *Ghusl Khāna,* which is a secret place where the second audience is given and the council sits. Into it only the principal Lords and officers of the court enter." Referring to the Royal establishment, Manucci says that " there is an officer styled Darogha Dó Cossa Choqui (Dārogha of the *Khāṣ* chaukī), that is, ' officer of the chosen sentinels ' ; the reason is that the company to which this name is given are all picked men and of the noblest families. Ordinarily they number 4,000 horsemen. This officer has charge of the Gousalcana (*Ghusl Khāna*)."

court chronicler, tells us the purpose of such a hall, and the names by which it was known :—

> "The Daulat Khāna-i-Khāṣṣ, by the wonderful art of expert artists and astonishing craftsmen, has been built between the *zanāna* apartment and the Dīwān-i-'Āmm, and the Lord, Possessor of the world, after leaving the Dīwān-i-'Āmm, honours that delightful house, and reposes on the royal throne. Here certain important affairs of state, which are not known except to confidants and court favourites, are settled by the problem-solving attention of the Emperor's heaven-like court, and angel-like power.
>
> As this prosperous house adjoins the Ḥammām, it is therefore known by the name of Ghusl-Khāna (a name which was given to such buildings in the time of His Majesty Akbar). In the (present) auspicious reign it is called Daulat Khāna-i-Khāṣṣ."[1]

Bernier states that "few are suffered to enter" the Dīwān-i-Khāṣṣ ; the *Umarās* were received therein by the King every evening, as in the morning at the Dīwān-i-'Āmm, and "were they remiss" in attendance something was retrenched from their pay.

The decoration of its ceiling is highly praised by native historians as well as by European travellers. Muḥammad Ṣāliḥ says that 9 *lacs* were spent on it.[2]

[1] *Bādshāh Nāma*, Vol. II, p. 220 ; *ibid.*, Vol. I, Part II, p. 237. Also see *'Amal-i-Ṣāliḥ*, fols. 579-80.

[2] *Op. cit.*, fol. 580.

Sayyid Aḥmad has the following account of this chamber :—

" To the north of the Khwābgāh, a big square (*Chauk*), is to be seen, and to the east of this, is a platform 1½ *gaz* high. In its centre is built the Dīwān-i-Khāṣṣ Palace.

Through its centre there flows the channel, called Nahr-i-Bihisht, which is 4 *gaz* wide. In the middle of this edifice, another room 18 *gaz* in length and 10 *gaz* in breadth, is made by erecting square columns with a platform in the centre. Cornelians, corals, and other precious stones are inlaid in the dado, in which flowers and foliage have also been carved.

From dado to ceiling it is ornamented with golden work. Its windows on the river side are closed by finely carved screens, the perforations of which are filled with glass. To the west of this there is a courtyard, 70 *gaz* by 60 *gaz*, round which rooms and arches of red sand-stone have been built, and to the west of this is an entrance which was connected with the Dīwān-i-'Āmm by a passage. In front of the entrance a red curtain is fixed up. At the time when the *darbār* is held, all the *Umarās* perform the ceremony of obeisance from this place. There is another gateway to the north of this courtyard leading to the Ḥayāt Bakhsh Garden, and to the south is a gateway leading to the entrance of the Royal Harem. In front of the central arch of this building, towards the courtyard

> a marble balustrade is erected. It is known by the name of *Chaukhandī-i-Dīwān-i-Khāṣṣ*. Its ceiling was of pure silver, but in the raids of the Marāṭhas and Jāṭs it was torn off."[1]

Aḥmad Shāh's contemporary historian says that, "it was from off the Dīwān-i-Khāṣṣ that Badu,[2] on account of his mean nature and the narrowness of his mind, took the silver of its ceiling, and turned it into money."[3] Keene (*Handbook to Delhi*, p. 131) states that the original ceiling was silver inlaid with gold at a cost of 39 *lacs* of rupees, which when looted and melted down by the Marāṭhas in 1760 realized 28 *lacs*. He adds in a footnote that this act of spoliation was perpetrated by them under Sadāshiv Rāo Bhāo, and in 1761, Aḥmad Shāh Durrānī inflicted on them a crushing defeat at Pānīpat. The hall had previously been despoiled in 1757 by Aḥmad Shāh, who among other plunders, took back with him a Mughal Princess as consort.

The following excellent description of the famous PEACOCK THRONE (*Takht-i-Ṭāūs*)[4] is given in the Bādshāh Nāma :—

> "Since from time immemorial and year in year out, various jewels of great price, each of

[1] *Athāru-ṣ-Ṣanādīd*. Cawnpore, 1904, Chapter II, pp. 41-42.

[2] Badu, probably Sadāshiv Rāo Bhāo, son of Chimājī and cousin of Peshwā Bālājī Bājī Rāo, slain in battle against Aḥmad Shāh Durrānī in 1761. T. W. Beale, *Biographical Dictionary*, p. 338.

[3] *Khazāna-i-'Āmirah*, p. 104.

[4] Some writers place the peacock throne in the Dīwān-i-'Āmm. Carr Stephen, however, is of the opinion that the throne stood on the marble *takht* at present in the Dīwān-i-Khāṣṣ. Bernier (Travels,

them worthy to be an ear-ring of Venus and to be set in a belt for the sun, had been kept in the Imperial Treasury, it occurred to the inspired mind (of the Emperor), in the early years of the beneficent reign, that the collection of such rare presents and accumulation of so many precious things, were only meant for the adornment of the Empire, and to increase its ornamentation. Therefore, they ought to be made use of in such a place that spectators might enjoy the world-enlightening beauty of the produce of the ocean and the mine, and that they should lend an added lustre to the Palace. Orders were issued that all kinds of rubies, diamonds, pearls and emeralds, the value of which was estimated at two hundred *lacs* of rupees, and in addition, those in the charge of the provincial treasury officers, should be brought for His Majesty's inspection, excepting only the Emperor's personal jewels, kept in the jewel office of the heaven-like palace.

p. 269) describes the throne, and in his description says "at the foot of the throne were assembled all the Omrahs in splendid apparel, upon a platform surrounded by a silver railing." Later he adds (Travels, p. 270), with reference to the court outside the building in which the throne stood, "as to the arcade galleries round the court, every Omrah had received orders to decorate one of them at his own expense, and there appeared a spirit of emulation who should best acquit himself to the Monarch's satisfaction. Consequently all the arcades and galleries were covered from top to bottom with brocade, and the pavements with rich carpets." The courtyard of the Dīwān-i-'Āmm would seem to be here referred to. Tavernier says the Great Mughal had seven magnificent thrones and that the principal throne stood in the hall of the first court, *i.e.*, the Dīwān-i-'Āmm.

Great and valuable jewels, the weight of which was fifty thousand *mithqāl*,[1] and the value of which was eighty-six *lacs* of rupees, were selected and entrusted to Bebadal Khān,[2] the superintendent of the goldsmiths' office, in order that the jewels might be studded in a slab made of one *lac* of *tolas* of pure gold, which is equal to two hundred and fifty thousand *mithqāls*, and the value of which was fourteen *lacs* of rupees. This slab was 3¼ by 2½ imperial *gaz* with a height of 5 *gaz*.

It was desired that the inside of the ceiling of the throne should be principally enamelled, and the rest set with jewels, and that the outside should be adorned with rubies and other precious stones. It was to be supported by twelve emerald coloured columns. Above the ceiling two images of peacocks, set in bright gems, were to be made, and between them a tree of rubies, diamonds, emeralds and pearls was to be fixed. To ascend the throne three steps studded with beautiful gems, were to be prepared.

In the course of seven years this heaven-like throne was completed at the cost of a hundred *lacs* of rupees, which is equal to three hundred

[1] The *mithqāl* is a weight equal to $1\frac{3}{7}$ drams.

[2] This mention of the officer to whom the work was entrusted shows that the statement of Mr. Beresford in his 'Guide to Delhi' that the Throne "was planned and executed under the supervision of Austin de Bordeaux" (see Carr Stephen, *Archæology of Delhi*, p. 231) is not substantiated by native historians. For Bebadal Khān, *vide Maāthiru-l-Umarā*, Persian Text, Vol. I, pp. 405-408.

and thirty-three thousand *tūmāns*[1] of 'Irāq, and to four crore *k͟hānī*, current in Transoxania (*Māwarāu-n-Nahr*).

Of the eleven slabs covered with jewels and erected around the throne for leaning against, the central one, on which the Emperor, a Solomon in rank, leans, by placing on it his truth-seeking hand, was valued at ten *lacs* of rupees. And of the jewels set in the throne, there was a ruby in the centre, valued at one *lac* of rupees, which S͟hāh 'Abbās,[2] King of Persia, had sent to His late Majesty[3] as a present by the hand of Zanbīl Beg. His late Majesty had sent it by 'Allāmī Afẓal K͟hān to the world-conquering Emperor, His Majesty the second Lord of the happy conjunction, as a reward for subduing the Deccan. At first, the sublime name of His Majesty, the Lord of happy conjunction,[4] the pole of the Faith and of Religion, and that of Mīrzā S͟hāh Ruk͟h, and Mīrzā Ulug͟h Beg, were written over it. After some time it fell into S͟hāh 'Abbās' hand, who also put his name on it, and when it was received by His late Majesty,

1 *Tumān*, a myriad; a sum of money equal to 10,000 Arabic silver *dirhams* which are about one-third less in value than those of the Greeks) and equivalent to fifteen dollars and a half.

2 S͟hāh 'Abbās of Persia (A. D. 1585-1628). He was a contemporary of the Emperor Jahāngīr.

3 The words *Jannat Makānī* are found in the text. It was a term used for Jahāngīr after his death and literally means, "nestling in paradise."

4 He refers to Tīmūr who is called "*Ṣāḥib Qirān*." Here the word *t͟hānī* is printed by mistake.

he added his own name with that of his illustrious father. Now it has received fresh light and brightness, and inestimable adornment from the exalted name of the King of the seven climes, and the Emperor of throne and crown."

The following verse, composed by *Ḥājī* Muḥammad Jān *Qudsī*,[1] the last line of which gives the date, was written by the order of the Emperor, in green enamelled work inside the throne :—

1. " How auspicious is the Imperial throne
   Which has been made ready by Divine help.
2. On the day when heaven desired to construct it,
   It first melted the gold of the sun.
3. By the order of the Emperor, the azure of the heaven,
   Was exhausted on its decoration.
4. What is the use of gold or of jewels but to decorate this throne ?
   It was the secret of the produce of ocean and mine.
5. On account of its ruby which is beyond value,
   The heart of the red-lipped beloved is uneasy.
6. Crowns, set with jewels, and rings, holding jewels in their eyes,[2]
   Waited for long (in the hope that they) might be set in its supports.

[1] *Qudsī* is his poetical name. He was *Maliku-Shu'arā* in Shāhjahān's time, and died in A. H. 1055 (A.D. 1645). See *Biographical Dictionary*, T. W. Beale, London, 1894.

[2] *i.e.*, the sockets for the jewels.

7. The world had become so short of gold on account of its use in the throne,
That the purse of the earth was empty of treasure.

8. Should the sky succeed in reaching the foot of the throne,
It will offer to it the sun and moon as a gift.

9. The august personage who rubbed his head on its base,
Had to add heaven as a step to (approach) the throne.

10. The tribute of ocean and mine is its robe:
The shadow of it is (like) the shelter of the Divine throne and seat.

11. It is decorated with various jewels:
Its every particle is a lamp to the world.

12. In its sides there are flowers of azure-like colour,
Shedding light like the lamp from Mount Sinai.

13. As his (Solomon's) hand could not reach it,
He set the precious stone of his ring on its steps.

14. A dark night by the lustre of its rubies and pearls
Can lend stars to a hundred skies.

15. As it kisses the foot of Shāhjahān,
So its rank is above the heavens.

16. The bestower of the world, and the prosperous king,
Spends the tribute of the whole earth on one throne.

17. Almighty Allah who exalted the heavenly
Throne and Seat,
Can make such a throne, through His
Divine Power.
18. As long as a trace remains of existence and
space,
Shāhjahān shall continue to sit on the
throne.
19. May such a throne be his seat every day,
Which has the tribute of seven climes under
one of its steps.
20. When the tongue asked the heart for its date,
It replied, " This is the throne of the Just
Emperor."[1]

The chronogram " *Aurang-i-Shāhinshāh-i-'Ādil* " gives the date A. H. 1044 (A. D. 1634).

It is well known that the Peacock Throne was taken to Persia[2] by Nādir Shāh in A. H. 1152 (A. D. 1739).[3]

[1] *Bādshāh Nāma*, Vol. I, Part II, pp. 78-81. Also see *Maāthiru-l-Umarā*, Vol. I, pp. 405-408.

[2] *Tārīkh Jahān Kushāi Nādirī*; also *Maāthiru-l-Umarā*, Vol. I, p. 408.

[3] The following extract from *Persia and the Persian question* (Vol. I, pp. 321-2) by the Hon. G. N. Curzon, M.P., will dispel at once the idea that the Peacock Throne of the 'Great Moghul' is still extant :—

" In this dilemma, but with the growing conviction that the modern Takht-i-Taous had a very shadowy connection, if any at all, with the plundered treasures of Delhi, I turned to contemporaneous records. I found in Malcolm (*History of Persia*, Vol. ii, p. 37), that Nadir Shah was so fond of the real Peacock Throne of the Great Mogul that he had an exact duplicate of it made in other jewels. This left two Peacock Thrones to be demolished between his death and the end of the last century, a catastrophe which in the anarchy and violence of those times would have been in itself no unlikely occurrence ; but it left the

The white marble daïs, on which it is said to have rested, was removed from the central room during the visit of the Prince of Wales in 1876 and placed in the east aisle of the hall where it now stands. (*Guide to Delhi*, Keene, p. 134.)

The entrance to the ḤAMMĀM, or baths, faces the north wall of the Dīwān-i-Khāṣṣ, the two rooms on either side being said by tradition to have been used as baths for the royal children. The baths consist of

Takht-i-Taous unexplained, as under no circumstances could the latter be described as duplicate of Tavernier's original. Now, however, I came across a passage in Fraser's 'Khorasan' in which he mentions that an old Kurd told him in 1822, that 'when Nadir Shah was murdered and his camp plundered, the Peacock Throne and the Tent of Pearls fell into our hands, and were torn in pieces and divided on the spot.' Any Kurd might certainly have been trusted to handle such an object as the Peacock Throne in the unceremonious manner here described, and, assuming the veracity of this particular Kurd, I witnessed with some delight the disappearance of the real Peacock Throne, or one of the two, from the scene.

A phrase in Morier's account had now set me thinking that the Takht-i-Taous at Tehran must be a modern structure after all. In the same passage which I have quoted in a footnote, he adds: 'It (*i.e.*, the throne) is said to have cost 100,000 *tomans*' (equivalent at the beginning of the century to about 100,000£)* ; herein clearly implying that an account or a tradition of its cost prevailed at Tehran, which was far more likely to be the case with a new than with an old fabric, and which was extremely unlikely to have been the case with an object carried off in plunder from a remote country seventy years before. At this stage, accordingly, I referred my doubts for solution to Tehran itself, and after an interval of some weeks was interested and (I may confess) rejoiced to hear, on the authority of the Grand Vizier and the former Minister for Foreign Affairs,† that, as I suspected, the Takht-i-Taous

* I understand, however, that it is now valued at nearly £200,000.

† When I was in Tehran I had in vain asked the same questions of the custodian of the treasury, and of every Persian official whom I met but without eliciting any satisfactory response.

three main apartments divided by corridors, the pavements, reservoirs, vapour slabs and walls, waist high, being of marble inlaid with vari-coloured stones. The apartment facing the river was known as the *Jāmakan*, the apartment wherein garments were removed, and contains two fountain basins, one for the use of the "rose-water spray" being of special interest. The marble lattice work of the window still exists, as do some of the old panes of coloured glass, too vivid in tone to be artistic. In the next apartment there is a central basin only. This could be used for hot or cold baths as desired. A marble couch of pleasing design still remains to show the character of the fittings

is not an Indian throne at all. It was constructed by Mohammed Husein Khan, Sadr or (High Priest) of Isfahan, for Fath Ali Shah when the latter married an Isfahan young lady, whose popular sobriquet, for some unexplained reason, was Taous Khanum, or the Peacock lady. The King is further said to have been so much delighted with the throne, that it was made a remarkably prominent feature in the ceremonies that commonly ensure upon marriage. Here, therefore, at one fell swoop, topples down the whole of the brilliant hypothesis, which has sustained scores of writers, and provided material for pages of glowing rhetoric. From the same authorities I learned that the original Peacock Throne of Nadir Shah (*i.e.*, the survivor of the two facsimiles) was discovered in a broken-down and piecemeal condition by Agha Mohammed Shah, who extracted it along with many others of the conqueror's jewels by brutal torture from his blind grandson Shah Rukh at Meshed, and then had the recovered portions of it made up into the throne of modern shape and style, which now stands at the end of the new Museum in the palace at Tehran, and to which I have alluded in my description of that apartment. In this chair, therefore, are to be found the sole surviving remnants of the Great Mogul's Peacock Throne, and the wedding present of Fath Ali Shah must descend from the position which it has usurped in the narrative of every writer in this century, without exception, who has alluded to it."

such chambers contained. The westernmost compartment, used for the hot baths only, possesses a vapour slab of singular beauty, the heating arrangements being in the west wall. Light was admitted to these two apartments by windows of stained glass as in the case of the east compartment. According to Shāh Nawāz Khān, the warm bath was inlaid with precious stones, and the square cold water reservoir adjoining had a jet of gold at each of its four corners. (*Guide to Delhi*, Keene, p. 130.) The baths were a favourite resort of the Mughal Emperors and in them business of a most important character was often transacted. Sir Thomas Roe visited Jahāngīr in the Ḥammām in the palace at Agra. In the cold season they were also used, being warmed by means of stoves. Sayyid Aḥmad states that the Ḥammām or baths in the Palace at Delhi were never used after the reigns of Shāhjahān and Aurangzeb. He adds that 125 *maunds* of firewood were required to heat them.

The body of the MOTĪ MASJID or Pearl Mosque measures some 40′ 0″ × 30′ 0″ and from floor to roof, 25′ 0″. Engrailed arches standing on a plinth 3½ feet high, support the roof of the building. The marble domes have replaced the original ones, covered with gilded copper. This material shared the same fate after the Mutiny (during which the mosque was damaged by a gun-shot) as that which covered the dome of the Muthamman Burj, and the *Chhatrīs* of the Dīwān-i-Khāṣṣ. The present marble domes, which were added after the Mutiny, are unfortunately out of proportion to the building. The original copper domes appear to have been considerably smaller. Carr Stephen gives

1070 A. H. (1659 A. D.) as the date of this building, while the contemporary historian of Aurangzeb gives 1073 A. H. as the date of the completion of the main structure, the decoration being finished a year later. Shāhjahān seems to have built no place of worship in the Fort and was wont to repair to the Jāmi' Masjid. The devout Aurangzeb, however, "always," as the historian says, "inclined to attend devotions,...... wished that, near the private bed-chamber, a small mosque should be built, and a graceful place of worship erected, so that at various times of the day and night, after a short walk from the blessed bed-chamber to the sacred place of worship, he might partake of the service of holy God and the worship of the Lord of Lords at his ease, and without the trouble of a retinue or long journey. Therefore to the north of the blessed Ghusl-Khāna, between the buildings of this beautiful and glorious palace, and its paradise-like garden (known by the name of Ḥayāt Bakhsh, a piece of land was selected for this noble edifice, and with the Divine assistance an auspicious mosque of white marble was built." The foundations were laid by the Emperor's orders on the 3rd day of Rabī'u-th-Thānī, while he "was shooting and hunting on the bank of the river Ganges." The date of the completion of this holy building—the abode of angels—was discovered by 'Āqil Khān, the ablest servant of the Court, in the following verse of the Qurān (*Sale's Translation of the Koran*, p. 468, London, 1857) :—

> "Verily the places of worship are set apart unto God ; wherefore invoke not any other therein, together with God."

The abovementioned chronogram was, the historian adds, approved by the Emperor, and "according to the supreme order it was carved in a stone slab in that holy place." The inscription is unfortunately no longer traceable.

There is a Motī Masjid (Pearl Mosque) in the Fort at Agra and another in the Fort at Lahore.

The HĪRĀ MAḤAL, the small marble pavilion immediately to the north of the baths, measures 22′ 5″ north and south by 19′ 5″ east and west, and has three open arches on each face. It was built by Bahādur Shāh II. The work shows the contrast in the quality of late Mughal architecture, as compared with that of the period of Shāhjahān.

The marble pavilion which lies on the south front of the SHĀH BURJ is of singular beauty, although already showing signs of the decadence in architecture which culminated in the reign of Aurangzeb. It measures some 63′ 3″ east and west by 32′ 0″ north and south. The centre of the north wall is occupied by a marble water cascade of pleasing design, which slopes into a 'scolloped' marble basin. For many years after the Mutiny the building served as an officer's residence, but in 1902 its conservation was taken up, the marble cascade being reconstructed and modern additions removed. The earthquake of 1904 so damaged the structure that it was necessary to take it almost entirely down and rebuild it. The *burj* behind the marble pavilion is an octagonal structure two storeys in height and formerly crowned by a domed cupola of similar design to that on the Asad Burj, which stands at the south-east corner of the Fort. In Lieutenant

Franklin's account of Delhi (*Asiatic Researches*) he says that in the "Shah Baug, or royal gardens, is a very large octagon room which looks towards the river Jumna. This room is called the Shah Boorj, or royal tower; it is lined with marble; and from the window of it the late Heir-apparent, Mirza Juwan Bukht (Jawān Bakht) made his escape in the year 1784, when he fled to Lucknow; and as the height is inconsiderable, effected it with ease." "A great part of this noble palace," adds the writer, "has suffered much by the destructive ravages of the late invaders. The Rohillas in particular, who were introduced by Gholaum Kauder (Ghulām Qādir) have stripped many of the rooms of their marble ornaments, and pavements, and have even picked out the stones from the borders of many of the floorings." (*Asiatic Researches*, Vol. IV, London, 1799.) They also passed three days digging up the floors for treasure which they supposed had been hidden by the Emperor Shāh 'Ālam in the Palace. The grass terrace between this pavilion and the Ḥammām was laid out as it now exists in 1911, and the Gun Battery, formerly in its centre, has now been removed (1914). The Nahr-i-Bihisht, the famous canal which supplied the many fountains and water channels of the Palace, also served this building and thence proceeded along the entire length of the east wall.

Keene (*Fall of the Moghul Empire*, p. 140) seems to infer that it was from the Salīmgaṛh that Jawān Bakht[1]

[1] Jawān Bakht was anxious to inform the British Governor, newly arrived at Lucknow, of the disorderly state of affairs at Delhi, consequent on the appointment of Afrāsyāb Khān, who had been created *Amīru-l-Umarā*, or premier noble of the realm, by Shāh 'Ālam, mainly through the instigation of the sister of the deceased premier, Mīrzā Najaf Khān.

escaped, after secretly departing from his chamber in the Palace and passing from the roof of one building to the roof of another until he reached the aqueduct (Nahr-i-Faiz̤, a canal of old foundation restored to use by S͟hāhjahān on his building the Fort) which crossed the garden Ḥayāt Bak͟hs͟h. "The night was stormy, and the prince suffering from fever, but he found a breach where the canal issued, by which he got to the rampart of the Salīmgaṛh. Here he descended by means of a rope and joined his friends on the river sands."

Bishop Heber, visiting Delhi in 1824-25, remarks on "a beautiful octagonal pavilion at the end of the terrace, also of marble, lined with the same mosaic flowers as in the room which I first saw, with a marble fountain in its centre, and a beautiful bath in a recess at one of its sides. The windows of this pavilion, which is raised to the height of the city wall, command a good view of Delhi and its neighbourhood.[1] But all was, when we saw it, dirty, lonely, and wretched; the bath and fountain dry; the inlaid pavement hidden with lumber and gardener's sweepings, and the walls stained with the dung of birds and bats." (*Heber's Journal*, Vol. II, London, 1828.)

The ASAD BURJ, situated on the south-east corner of the Fort, is of similar design to the S͟hāh Burj but without a fronting marble pavilion, and was much damaged in 1803, when the city was defended by Colonel Ochterlony against Harnāth C͟hela. It was considerably repaired by Akbar II.

[1] The *C͟hhatrī* on the roof was apparently taken to Meerut some 28 years ago and re-erected over a well there.

Only one-half of the original area of this garden exists at present, its western portion being occupied by the military barracks. The garden was bounded on the north and south by a range of buildings with the 'Sāwan' and 'Bhādon' pavilions as the central features, while terminating the ends of the main causeways, running east and west from the central tank, were other marble pavilions, that on the east terrace being known as the Motī Maḥal.[1] West again of the Ḥayāt Bakhsh gardens lay the Maḥtāb Bāgh (garden of moonlight), and this extended up to the line of the arcaded street running northwards from the square in front of the Naubat Khāna (see page 8). The site of this last-named garden is now the barrack square and, although all its pavilions have gone, it is more than probable that a clearance of the surface earth will reveal traces of the old parterres and water causeways. The Indian historian's account of the Ḥayāt Bakhsh garden will be of interest.

"This Iram-like[2] Ḥayāt Bakhsh garden, which, by the display of its beautiful flower-beds, of the various green plants, and blessed flowers, and by the running water channels facing the garden, in the name of Holy God, *is* a garden. The wave of its fresh grass has surpassed the roses, and the fruitful trees of diverse kinds are interlaced with each other in such a way

[1] This pavilion has disappeared, only a few traces of its foundations coming to light on the removal of the Gun Battery which stood till recently at this spot. It is shown in old drawings of the east wall of the Fort.

[2] Iram is the name of a fabulous garden, famous in eastern poetry. It is said to have been planned by Shāddād, son of 'Ād, in emulation of the gardens of Paradise.

that the sky is not anywhere visible beneath them. Especially does the tank in its centre, which is 60 *gaz* by 60 *gaz*, shine as a sun-like mirror with its waving light, and it is decorated with forty-nine silver jets, besides 112 more jets which play round it. In all its four avenues, each of which is made of red sandstone, and completed with a breadth of 20 *gaz*, there is a channel 6 *gaz* broad, which flows with 30 playing fountains in its centre. At the left and right (sides) of this garden two charming buildings (*Sāwan*[1] and *Bhādon*[2]) decorated with pictures and paintings like the enamelled throne of the Queen of *Shaiba*, or like Solomon's throne studded with emeralds, have been built. Through the two water-ways of the tanks which are made in the centre of these buildings, the water is constantly bursting forth gracefully, and from the edge of their platforms, which have the height of $1\frac{1}{2}$ *gaz* (from the ground), it falls into the tank below in the form of a cascade. In the niches, flower-vases of gold and silver, full of golden flowers, are placed during the daytime, and at night, white wax candles which appear like the stars in the thin clouds, are lighted and placed inside the veil of water."[3]

Bishop Heber says " the gardens are not large, but, in their way, must have been extremely beautiful. They are full of very old orange and other fruit trees,

[1] *Sāwan*, a Hindī month corresponding to July and August, the first month of the rainy season.

[2] *Bhādon*, a Hindī month corresponding to August and September, the second month of the rainy season.

[3] '*Amal-i-Ṣāliḥ*, Fols. 580-82. Sayyid Aḥmad gives the same description, and it is very likely that the above work is his real source. (*Āthāru-ṣ-Ṣanādīd*, Chapter II, pp. 45-48, Cawnpore, 1904.)

with terraces and parterres, on which many rose bushes were growing, and even now (January), a few jonquils in flower."

The Ẓafar Maḥal—the red sandstone pavilion in the centre of the main tank—was built by Bahādur Shāh II, the last Mughal Emperor, Ẓafar being his poetical name.

Sayyid Aḥmad in his account of this building says that, "on one side a bridge for ingress and egress has been built."[1] This has disappeared, and the pavilion has now little to commend it to notice.

The same historian also writes: "In the middle of this garden (the Ḥayāt Bakhsh) a large canal flows very pleasantly. His Exalted Majesty Sirāju-d-Din Muḥammad Bahādur Shāh has now made a *jharna*[2] of red stone near the canal towards the west, like that of the Quṭb Ṣāḥib,[3] and the garden has been much improved by this. In this garden there is a holy footprint (Qadam Sharīf)."[4]

To the south[5] of the Ḥayāt Bakhsh garden stood a small mosque—a later addition—commonly known as the "Chobī Masjid" or Wooden Mosque. It existed up to the time of the Mutiny of 1857, as we find it

[1] *Āthāru-ṣ-Ṣanādīd*, Chapter II, p. 20, Lucknow, 1878.

[2] *Jharna*, a kind of shower bath, or water-fall.

[3] The author is perhaps referring to the chute in the Jharna Garden at Mehrauli, to which the Emperor added some buildings.

[4] *Op. cit.*, Lucknow, 1874, Chapter II, p. 21. It should be remembered that "Qadam Sharīf," literally a sacred foot, here means the footprint of the Prophet. Most probably it is the same which was kept in the Delhi Municipal Museum and was recently removed to the Delhi Museum of Archæology, see Nos. C. 28 and 29, *Museum Catalogue*.

[5] See the old map of the Fort in the Delhi Museum of Archæology No. K. 2.

mentioned in Sayyid Aḥmad's work, but no trace of it is now left. It is described in the following words :—

" This mosque was built by King Aḥmad Shāh in A. H. 1164 (A. D. 1750), and being supported by columns and arches of wood, was known by the name " Chobī Masjid."

" It was entirely ruined, but was re-built in A. H. 1267 (A. D. 1850) at Government expense."[1]

On the entrance of the mosque was the following inscription[2] :—

" This mosque was built by the King, Protector of the faith
Who received help from Divine power.
Whoever performs the prostrations of supplication there
Is sure to be guided by the light of worship.
The foot of wisdom slipped in astonishment
When he began to deliberate upon the date.
The angel, though very pride, was thus inspired :
'The mosque of Aḥmad has attained the rank of the Zodiac sign.

Year 1164.' "

The history of the CANAL, by which Shāhjahān brought water to the Fort from a point thirty *kos* [3]

[1] *Op. cit.*, Cawnpore, 1904, Chapter III, p. 92.

[2] This inscription is taken from *Miftāḥu-t-Tawārīkh*, T. W. Beale, p. 332, where it is compared with that recorded in *Āthāru-s-Sanādīd*, Lucknow, 1874, Chapter II, p. 21.

[3] A *kos* is roughly equal to 2¼ miles.

higher up the river[1] is of no little interest, and is thus traced by the authors of *Maāthiru-l-Umarā* and *'Amal-i-Ṣāliḥ*. To the canal he gave the name Nahr-i-Bihisht.[2] It is said that it was originally the work of Fīroz Shāh Khaljī in A. H. 691 (1291 A. D.) and that he brought the canal from the Jumna near Khizrābād to Safaidūn,[3] his hunting ground, a distance of 30 *kos* from its starting point. After his death it became dry but was cleared by Shihābu-d-Din Aḥmad Khān, Governor of Delhi in the time of Akbar. He rechristened the canal Nahr-i-Shihāb after himself, and used it for bringing water to his estate in A. H. 969 (1561 A. D.). It again became neglected, but in A. H. 1048 (1638 A. D.) Shāhjahān ordered it to be cleared as far as Safaidūn and brought thence to the Fort at Delhi.[4] Sayyid Aḥmad in his description states that "it had become dry again, but that in A. H. 1236 (1820 A. D.), it was repaired and cleared by order of Government and from that time it continues to run for the common benefit."[5]

[1] *Maāthiru-l-Umarā*, Vol. III, p. 466. See also *Āthāru-ṣ-Ṣanādīd*, Cawnpore ed., Chap. II, p. 54.

[2] *'Amal-i-Ṣāliḥ*. Fol. 579.

[3] Safaidūn is shown on the map about 65 miles north-west by north of Delhi, in Jind State.

[4] *Maāthiru-l-Umarā*, Vol. III, pp. 465-6.

[5] The chronology of this canal, now known as the Western Jumna Canal, with its dependent branches serving Ambala, Karnal, Hissar, Rohtak, Delhi and parts of the Native States of Patiala, Jind and Bikanir is given as follows in the *History and description of Government Canals in the Punjab* by Mr. J. J. Hatten (Lahore, Punjab Government Press, pp. 1-3) :—

A. D. 1351.—The Emperor Firoz Shah utilised the Chautang Naddi to conduct water to Hansi and Hissar.

About A. D. 1468.—Water ceased to flow beyond the lands of Kaithal, near Karnal.

SALĪMGAṚH was built by Salīm S͟hāh, son and successor of S͟her S͟hāh, as a defence against the approach of Humāyūn (1546 A. D.), the whole circuit of the walls being about three quarters of a mile. Originally protected by nineteen bastions and said to have cost 4 *lacs*, it was still unfinished at Salīm S͟hāh's death in 1552, and was, thereafter, consigned to neglect. Carr Stephen (*Archæology of Delhi*, p. 195) states that "eighty years later (*i.e.*, after the death of Salīm S͟hāh) Farīd K͟hān, otherwise known as Murtaẕā K͟hān, an Amīr who flourished in the reigns of Akbar and

A. D. 1568.—The Emperor Akbar re-excavated the work of Firoz and brought a supply from the Jumna and the Somb into the Chautang on to Hansi and Hissar. A valuable *sanad* by Akbar on this work exists.

About A. D. 1626.—Ali Mardan, the famous engineer of the Emperor Shahjahan, drew a canal to Delhi, first by way of Gohana, along a natural depression now occupied by a main drain, and when this failed, by way of Panipat and Sonipat. The cost of this work is reported to have been very great, and considerable engineering skill was shown.

A. D. 1707.—Water ceased to reach Hariana (Hansi-Hissar).

1740.—Flow ceased at Safaidon on Firoz Shah's line.

1755-1760.—Delhi branch ceased to flow, owing to political disturbances and the difficulties experienced in efficient maintenance, especially at the head.

1810.—First surveys made by British Government for a restoration of the Delhi branch.

1817.—Captain Blair appointed to restore the Delhi branch.

1819.—Delhi branch reopened.

1820.—Water once more entered Delhi.

1823.—Restoration of the Hansi Branch (Firoz's) began.

1825.—Hansi branch reopened, etc., etc.

Of the earlier schemes little need be said. Firoz Shah's canal by which the Hansi branch, below Datrat, was known, was little more than a monsoon supply channel, which was led down a drainage bed to the tanks at Hansi and Hissar, the royal residences.

Jahāngīr, seems to have obtained Salīmgaṛh, with other possessions along the banks of the Jumna, in grant from Akbar, and he built houses in this fort." In 1828 these buildings were in a complete state of ruin, but a two-storeyed pavilion and a well-stocked garden were still preserved with care by Akbar II, who occasionally used to take an airing here undisturbed by the public. It was here in August 1788

Akbar's canal was undoubtedly a perennial channel. The two ancient bridges at Karnal and Safaidon testify to this, and there is no reason to doubt the genuineness of the *sanad*, by Akbar, which is dated Shawwal A. H. 978, Firozpur, where Akbar was at the time. This *sanad* clearly states that the water was to be obtainable "All the year round." The existence of a complete system of water-courses points to the same fact. No such water-courses existed in the channel brought down by Firoz.

'Ali Mardan's canal was indeed a great engineering undertaking. The river supply coming down the right bank of the Jumna was bunded up annually at Fatehgarh near Dadupur, about 14 miles below Tājawala. The line followed was the drainage at the foot of the high land (*bangar*) of the right bank. Several cuts through the high land had to be made. Drainage and escapes were fairly provided for. The "Poolchaddar aqueduct near Delhi taking the canal over the Najafgaṛh *jhil* drain, and acting at the same time as a waste weir, was a great engineering feat at the time. The total length of the aqueduct is 80 feet. Thickness of canal floor 3½ feet, waterway 16 feet at bed, and 19 feet at top of parapets, which were 5 feet 9 inches high—all carried on massive 8 feet thick piers with cut-waters and arches 8 feet span over the drainage. This work was repaired by the British Government with slight modifications when the branch was opened to Delhi in 1820. The water rate appears to have been regulated by the time that the outlets remained open. It is stated that 1,000 armed peons and 500 horses were maintained on the establishment. The net revenue from the canals was reckoned equal to the maintenance of 12,000 horses." Further information on the history of the Canal of 'Alī Mardān Khān will be found in the *Memoranda on the Western Jumna Canal, North Western Provinces*, by Major W. E. Baker, Superintendent of Canals, North Western Provinces; London, 1849. In it are also given drawings of several of the old Mughal aqueducts. The Poolchaddar aqueduct is no longer used. It lies close to the modern Najafgaṛh *jhil* aqueduct, just outside Delhi, and is now maintained as an historical building.

that the helpless Emperor Shāh ʻ Ālam was imprisoned after being blinded by the Rohilla brigand, Ghulām Qādir (Keene, p. 19), and some months afterwards the latter escaped through Salīmgaṛh with his followers, crossing the five-arched bridge which connected it with Lāl Qilaʻ, or the fort of Shāhjahānābād. The bridge, built by Jahāngīr to connect Salīmgaṛh with the main land, was demolished to make way for the present railway bridge, but an inscription from it is still preserved in the Museum. The translation is as follows :—

> "By the order of the King of the seven climes, the Emperor (who rules) with equity, justice and good government,
>
> Jahāngīr, the son of Emperor Akbar, whose sword has subdued the world.
>
> When this bridge was built in Delhi, the praises of which cannot be expressed,
>
> For the date of its completion wisdom spoke thus : ʻ The bridge of the Emperor of Delhi (named) Jahāngīr.ʼ "

The value of the letters of this chronogram (*Pul-i-Shāhinshah-i-Dehlī Jahāngīr*) is equal to A. H. 1031 (A. D. 1621).

The meaning of the words placed in the margin of the original inscription is as follows : (God is great.) (Great in His Glory) (O ! the Most Victorious.) (O ! Helper.) (O ! Bounteous.) (O ! Immortal.) (In the year 17) (of the accession) (of Jahāngīr) (Under the management) (of Husain Ḥalabī). (Written by Sharīf.)

Another inscription, said to have been on the east side of the bridge, is recorded by Sayyid Aḥmad, the translation being as follows :—

"God is Great."

"It was built by the order of King Nūru-d-Dīn Jahāngīr, the Great. The year and auspicious date (of its erection is found in the following chronogram) : *Ān Ṣirāṭu-l-Mustaqīm.* 'That (is the) right path.' A. H. 1031."

The Fort during the Mutiny.

The following account has been principally abstracted from Fanshawe's *Delhi Past and Present, The Siege of Delhi in 1857* by Lieutenant-General Handcock, *Seven Cities of Delhi* by Gordon Hearn, *Indian Mutiny Papers, Trial of Bahādur S͟hāh,* and *Two Native narratives of the Mutiny in Delhi,* translated by C. T. Metcalfe, C.S.I. Only such events as are connected with the Palace have been mentioned.

It would appear from the various accounts that Bahādur S͟hāh II held daily *darbārs* in the Fort during the occupation of Delhi by the mutineers, these ceremonies being attended by the principal residents of Delhi and officers of the mutinied troops. Questions regarding the payment of the troops, levying of taxes on the inhabitants for this object, and reports on the state of the fighting were discussed, while letters were written to induce others to join in the revolt. Suspected spies or traitors were also dealt with and *nazars* (*lit. Presents*) presented. The Emperor seems to have been, from the first, treated with but scant ceremony, his orders being generally disregarded, while when the question of the occupation of the city by the English became only a matter of days the Palace became completely disorganised.[1]

On the 11th May 1857 the sepoys from the mutinied regiments at Meerut arrived at Delhi and clamoured for admittance to the Palace, declaring that they had killed the English at Meerut and had come to fight for the true faith. Captain Douglas, commandant of the palace guard, wished to go down and speak to them, but being dissuaded by the Emperor, Bahādur S̲h̲āh II, he contented himself with addressing them from the balcony of the Mut̲h̲amman Burj. He was, however, defied, and the sepoys of the palace guard, furnished by the 38th Native Infantry, admitted the mutineers. Captain Douglas then proceeded with the civil authorities to the Calcutta gate of the city in order to interview the rebels, but the party was attacked by the sepoys who had effected an entrance by the water gate, and obliged to retreat to the Lahore gate of the Palace. The Native Infantry on guard refused to fire on the

[1] The mutineers, cavalry and infantry, occupied the Ḥayāt Bak̲h̲s̲h̲ garden and the Mahtāb Bag̲h̲, injuring them considerably. Magazine stores were kept by them in the Dīwān-i-K̲h̲āṣṣ, while they spread their bedding in the same building. Repeated orders were given by the King to the rebel troops not to occupy the royal farrās̲h̲k̲h̲āna, and the regiment of cavalry were also told frequently to evacute the gardens. "These," said the King, "were places which not even Nādir S̲h̲āh or Aḥmad S̲h̲āh or any of the British Governor-Generals of India ever entered on horseback." The troops also galloped up to the Hall of Audience and the *Jalwa k̲h̲āna* (*Jilaukhāna*, see p. 21), wearing caps instead of turbans.

mutineers, and Mr. Simon Fraser, Commissioner at Delhi, remonstrated with them for their behaviour; he then turned to mount the steps leading to Captain Douglas's rooms. As he placed his foot on the first step, two men, named "Kārlik Beg" and "Mughal Beg," rushed forward and cut him down. In another account Ḥājī, a lapidary, is cited as the murderer of Mr. Fraser. Captain Douglas, already wounded in the ankle, had been carried upstairs in a fainting condition, but, on recovering, gave orders for all doors and windows to be closed. The others in the room were Mr. Jennings, the Chaplain, and a friend, two married ladies, and two girls, Miss Jennings and Miss Clifford, who had been conveyed to the Begam's Palace for protection. The doors were then broken in and all the occupants immediately cut to pieces. The same day two *ṣūbedārs* were admitted to a private audience with the Emperor as the representatives of the crowds of rebel soldiery, and protested that they would "bring the revenue of the whole Empire to the King's treasury." The news of the death of some more officers then reached the Palace, followed by the arrival of a regiment of cavalry who took up their position in the court of the Dīwān-i-Khāṣṣ. Many of the men forcibly intruded themselves into the presence of the Emperor, and the interior of the Fort became a scene of the wildest confusion. Orders were issued by Ḥakīm Aḥsānullah Khān to the Princes to assume command of the several regiments. Throughout the whole of the 12th May the Palace was thronged with soldiers demanding pay. Formerly a silver throne had been kept in the Hall of Special Audience on which the King used to take his seat on special occasions of State; but since the year 1842 the presentation of the usual offering by the Agent to the Governor General on occasion of salutes and interviews had been disallowed. This throne was then removed and placed in a recess in the passage behind the King's sitting room, and since that time was in disuse till the 12th May 1857, when it was brought out again, and the King took his seat on it, as on a throne. The Emperor also left the Fort and proceeded through the city on an elephant to allay the fears of the inhabitants. On his return, he found the court of the Dīwān-ī-Khāṣṣ again full of soldiers, and pointed out to some of the *ṣūbedārs* that, hitherto, the enclosure had been sacred to Royalty alone, and never entered forcibly by armed men. In the evening of the same day he again had cause to complain of disrespect, being addressed by some "*Are Bādshāh! Are Buḍḍhe!*" ("I say, King; I say, you old man"); while others caught him by the hand or touched his beard. Thirty persons had taken refuge in the underground apartments of the Rāja of Kishangaṛh, and on the 13th May a few of these escaped, but were recaptured and taken to the Palace. It is said that the King ordered that all the captives should be sent thither, but his orders were disregarded. On May 14th the Emperor was so distracted by the turmoil going on around him that he refused audience to all. He ordered a search to be made for the bodies of Mr. Fraser and Captain Douglas, that they might be interred in the Christian burial ground, while the other bodies were to be thrown into the river.

On May 16th, a large number of mutineers assembled before the Palace and threatened the Emperor, accusing him of concealing some forty Europeans. They threatened to abduct Zīnat Maḥal, the Queen, and hold her as a hostage for the Emperor's loyalty. On this day, at about 9-30 or 10 A.M., all the Europeans in the Palace, forty-nine in number, principally women and children,[1] were murdered in cold blood near a tank in the centre of the square before the Naubat Khāna. The Palace on May 21st was crowded with a howling mob of men demanding pay.

Bahādur Shāh II left the Palace on the 25th and proceeded to the Jāmi' Masjid for prayer. The next day a discovery was made that some one had filled the guns in the Salīmgaṛh with *kankar* and stone. Ḥakīm Ahsānullah Khān was suspected and narrowly escaped with his life.

An unnamed European, dressed as a Hindū fortune teller, and "carrying an almanack," was brought into the Palace on the 29th and murdered.

On May 30th news was received that the mutineers had been defeated by the English at the Hindan, and numbers of wounded men appeared in the city. The Emperor held a court at night and was much perplexed at the turn affairs had taken.

News of the murder of the English at Bareilly reached the Palace on the 31st, and on the same day the King issued orders that he would no longer receive any petitions in person, but that they must be sent to Maḥbūb 'Alī Khān and Ḥakīm Aḥsānullah Khān.

[1] It is said that there were only five or six men among them. 100 or 150 ruffians were employed in the work in murder.

News reached the Palace that the Lieutenant-Governor of Agra had been informed of the events at Delhi.

A levée was held on the 3rd June attended by "all the nobles of the city." Some Mughals also presented themselves and asked permission to raise the flag of *Jihād* (Religious War).

The son of one Pīyā Mal Malsūrī was seized on June 8th, and brought before the Emperor, his father being suspected of providing the English with supplies. The next day a petition was sent to the Palace for his release on the ground that Pīyā Mal had supplied the mutineers with provisions daily and in no way befriended the English.

On June 10th the Emperor issued a proclamation for the forcible opening of all the shops in the city. The mutineers lost heavily in an engagement on the same day, while some 100 English were killed. Their heads were cut off and paraded through the city. Fifty sepoys seized Rāja Ajīt Singh of Patiala and brought him as a prisoner before the Emperor. He was threatened with death unless he used his influence with his brother, who was in league with the English. The Rāja threw himself at the Emperor's feet and implored his protection, and, it being explained that there had been a difference between the brothers for some time, his immediate release was ordered.

On June 11th the Emperor ordered one hundred *maunds* of gunpowder to be prepared, being cheered by the marksmanship of one Qūlī Khān, an artillery man, who kept up a constant fire on the English. A confidential report was received that the Queen of England, on receipt of news of the Mutiny, had ordered the despatch of 24,000 troops. The next day one Piyāre Lāl was taken forcibly before the Emperor and charged with supplying sulphur to the English. Bahādur Shāh expressed displeasure at the failure of the mutineers to drive off the English.

On June 14th a *mahāwat*, who had deserted with his elephant from the English camp, made his way to the Palace, and the elephant was appropriated by the Emperor for his own use. The next day seven cannon balls fell into the Palace. The Emperor threatened to leave Delhi and retire to the Qutb unless the troops left the city.

On June 17th 'seven carts with lime' were despatched for the repairs of Salīmgaṛh, while a cannon which had been lying at the door of the Palace since the time of Shāhjahān, was mounted at the Lahore gate. "It being a long range gun, it was intended to annoy the English troops marching from Agra."

An audience was held on the 20th and attended by the officers of the Naṣīrābād regiments who had mutinied on the 22nd ; three regiments also arrived from Jullundhur. Their officers attended the audience and complained that they had been attacked by Patiala troops. They boasted that they had killed the Collector of Naṣīrābād and had taken his elephant, which they brought with them. The Emperor said that they were "Great *Bahādurs*, whose like was not to be met with".

The next day the gun of the time of Shāhjahān was mounted.[1] Qūlī Khān, who has already been referred

[1] *Two native narratives of the mutiny.*—It appears from the text as if this was a different gun from the one previously mentioned.

to, was brought before the Emperor on the 24th and charged with being in collusion with the English. Some of his shots had apparently gone astray and killed some of the mutineers. A large *darbār* was held on the 25th at which Bahādur Shāh received reports of the state of affairs. He addressed the *sardārs* of the sepoys and pointed out to them that they were destroying the kingdom that had lasted 500 years, adding that after an engagement with the English they always returned "topsy turvy". He expressed the wish that they should all leave the city, and the following day issued a general order to this effect.

On the 28th the leading inhabitants waited on the Emperor to pay their respects. A man caught digging a mine in the Palace, in connivance with the English. was blown from a gun at Salīmgaṛh. Little of importance happened during the next two days save the arrival of some 500 'fanatics,' who presented an elephant they had taken from the English.

On July 2nd Muḥammad Bakht Khān, a Bareilly mutineer, was appointed Commander-in-Chief, and he seems to have been given full control, not only of the army but of the civil administration.

On the 3rd he attended at the Palace accompanied by "two European sergeants who had accompanied his force from Bareilly and made themselves very useful". They had also, it was stated, prevented the Europeans at Bareilly blowing away natives from guns. They were ordered to report on the various batteries. Nothing worthy of especial remark occurred within the next few days in the Palace. The daily audience was thronged by those who complained of being plundered by the mutineers. On the 6th a man at Salīmgaṛh had his head taken off by a cannon ball; an order was issued that youths without turbans and all armed men were to be henceforth excluded from the Dīwān-i-Khāṣṣ. A levée was held in the Dīwān-i-'Āmm on the 8th. The next day several Europeans, who were found concealed in the *sarāi* of Maḥbūb 'Alī Khān, were decapitated and their heads laid before the Emperor, who gave a reward of 100 rupees to the murderers.

On the 10th Bahādur Shāh visited the battery at Salīmgaṛh. On the 13th he entered the Dīwān-i-Khāṣṣ through the "Khāṣpura" gate and "all the nobles of Delhi and officers of the army paid their respects." A regimental band was in attendance, and received two gold *mohurs* for their services. Five hundred ladders were prepared by the orders of Muḥammad Bakht Khān, so that the sepoys could escape over the wall in the event of the English entering the city. On the 18th the Emperor entered the Dīwān-i-'Āmm and received the salutations of the nobles who were present. The next day he visited Salīmgaṛh. He was also informed by the Commander-in-Chief that an English sergeant and two English soldiers had been executed in the river bed. The King, as if under a divine inspiration, suddenly said, "If I be altogether victorious, I shall go to Agra after the victory and make a pilgrimage to Ajmer and visit the tomb of Salīm Chīshtī (?)." On the 20th he inspected the property of some murdered Europeans and ordered it to be made over to the Begam. He visited

Salīmgaṛh the following day and inspected a newly raised regiment, which was given the number 56. The *darbār* of the 22nd was the occasion of a complaint by Ba<u>kh</u>t <u>Kh</u>ān regarding a rumour in circulation to the effect that he was in league with the English, and was in the habit of "slinking home and leaving his men to fight without orders." The Emperor assured him that he trusted him, and "that he (the King) had no cause for enmity with the English, but felt that he would be exalted by the army that had rushed to his protection." The Princes, on this occasion, took exception to the actions of the Commander-in-Chief who whispered in the King's ear in their presence. The General apologised with flattery to the Princes and the matter was dropped. On the 23rd the Emperor visited Salīmgaṛh, while an elephant, brought in by the landholders of Kalanaur (?), was presented to him and sent to the royal stables.

He again inspected Salīmgaṛh on the 28th and afterwards held a *darbār* in the Dīwān-i-'Āmm. "There was a great gathering of officers." Ḥakīm Aḥsānullah <u>Kh</u>ān demurred to one of the Emperor's orders regarding the killing of cows during the *'Id*, and the Emperor closed the audience in anger. The audience on the 30th was marked by a somewhat similar incident. "The son of Nawāb Muḥammad Mīr <u>Kh</u>ān was seated during the audience; after Bahādur <u>Sh</u>āh had left, Mīr Sayyid 'Alī <u>Kh</u>ān said to him: "It is very improper that you should remain seated whilst all other nobles stand, and you, too, must stand in future, and not take a seat, else it will not go well with you." At the audience of August 2nd the Emperor recited the following verses which he had composed and sent to Ba<u>kh</u>t <u>Kh</u>ān :—

> "May all the enemies of the Faith be killed today;
> The Firangīs be destroyed, root and branch!
> Celebrate the festival of the *'Īd-i-Qurbān* by great slaughter:
> Put our enemies to the edge of the sword, slay, and spare not!"

The same evening the officers were attempting to raise the hopes of the Emperor, and exclaimed, "by the help of God, we shall take the Ridge yet. At that moment a round shot from the English entered Salīmgaṛh and killed a sepoy."

On the 7th, while the Emperor was in the Salīmgaṛh Fort, he received news that the sepoys were coming to plunder the Palace. He was standing in the porch of the gateway at the time and at that moment some sepoys arrived in search of Aḥsānullah <u>Kh</u>ān who was suspected of being in league with the English. Bahādur <u>Sh</u>āh commanded Ḥasan 'Alī <u>Kh</u>ān, also suspected of treachery, to be hidden behind the throne in the throne room, while Aḥsānullah <u>Kh</u>ān was to be taken to the "underground place for worship,"[1] and it was explained to the sepoys that he was not in the Palace. After some time they returned and demanded that he should be given up to them. This was refused at first, but the Ḥakīm was eventually handed over to them and confined in the room kept for the custody of the crown jewels.[2]

[1] This place has not yet been identified.
[2] To the north of the Dīwān-i-'Āmm court.

On August 8th, the Begam sent word to Bahādur Shāh that she, too, was suspected in being in league with the English, and she had been warned that the sepoys intended to plunder the Palace. Ḥakīm Aḥsān-ullah Khān was released on the 10th and restored to favour. In an audience held on the 13th the Emperor objected to the wearing of pistols in his presence. On the 15th three hundred sepoys, "despairing of their pay and disheartened at the result of the rebellion, brought in their fire-arms and left the city through the Calcutta gate for their own homes."

The Emperor held a council of war in the Salīmgaṛh Fort on the 18th. On the 21st Bakht Khān brought some elephants and horses for his inspection, and he went at once to the porch of the gate of the Palace and selected seventeen horses. Salīmgaṛh was visited the next day and the battery there ordered to fire a few rounds, Bahādur Shāh remarking that it was to be regretted that instead of the fire of the English being silenced their batteries were getting nearer every day. The gunners replied, "No fear, your Majesty; we are getting the better of them." On the 23rd the same battery was ordered to elevate their guns so as to reach the English camp. The heads of five Englishmen, killed at Indore, were brought before the King. General Bakht Khān was accused by his officers of negotiating with the English and orders were issued that he was not to be admitted to the Palace. Several foot soldiers attended the *darbār* and complained that no opium could be purchased in the bazar.

On the 24th the Emperor visited Salīmgaṛh where some excavations for buried treasure were in progress.

Nothing was, however, found, save some small field pieces. The following day he went on the river and watched the artillery fire directed on the English from the Fort.

More demands were made for pay by deputations of officers and Bahādur S͟hāh offered them some of the crown jewels which they refused, saying that they were satisfied of his willingness to give up his life and property to sustain them.

On the 31st of August the coat and shoes of the Prophet Muḥammad were brought to the Palace from the Mosque of Nulub-u-Din (*sic*).

The daily *darbār* continued throughout the first half of September, being generally thronged by sepoys demanding their pay, or by the unfortunate inhabitants of the city who were being freely robbed. On September 4th, Sir Thomas Metcalfe's house at the Qutb was plundered and the property brought to the Emperor. He was much displeased as he had appointed servants for its safe custody. Whether he intended to take it for himself or protect it out of a friendly feeling for the owner is a matter of speculation. The local jewellers were brought in a body to the Palace on the 7th and were informed that 8 *lacs* of rupees must be immediately forthcoming for the troops, while on the following day the police proceeded to collect three months' rent from all the inhabitants of the city. Much of the money intended for the troops appears about this time, to have been appropriated by the Princes. Reference is again made to Bahādur S͟hāh repairing, during these days, to the "underground mosque." Several proclamations were issued that he would lead an attack in person against the English and that all citizens, irrespective of caste, were to take the field. It was rumoured on the 14th that the English would assault the city, and the Emperor remained in his private apartments. The assault, as is well known, actually took place and was successful. The 15th, 16th, 17th and 18th were spent in clearing the mutineers out of the ground between the town walls and Palace, and in shelling the latter and Salīmgaṛh, which was still occupied by the enemy.

On the 19th Bakht Khān represented to the Emperor that his only safety lay in flight, and begged him to accompany him and renew war in the open country. Bahadur Shāh, however, allowed the army to depart without him and took refuge in the tomb of Humāyūn. On the same day the Lahore gate of the Palace, which appeared to be deserted save for an occasional gun shot fired at the troops at the end of the Chāndī Chauk, was blown in. The 4th Punjab Infantry broke the chain of the inner gate by firing muskets close to it, and charged down the vaulted passage (the *Chhatta Chauk*) into the Palace. A single sentry remained in the passage and fired at Lieutenant McQueen, but the bullet went through that officer's helmet only. Shortly after the Palace had been entered from this side Lieutenant Aikman, V. C., also of the 4th Infantry, entered it from Salīmgaṛh, again meeting a solitary sentry only. It was found to be deserted save for some fanatics and wounded sepoys who were quickly disposed of. Headquarters were established in the Palace, which was held by the 60th Rifles and the Kumaun battalion. Major Wilson's personal guard was drawn from the Sirmur Gurkhas, as a compliment to that gallant regiment. On the 21st Lieutenant Hodson captured the Emperor a few miles south of the city, and on the following day two of his sons were taken at the tomb of Humāyūn and summarily shot. On the 21st a royal salute was fired in honour of the capture of the city, and on Sunday, the 27th, a thanksgiving service was held in the Dīwān-i-Khāṣṣ. The following January the Emperor of Delhi was brought to trial in the same building, and, after an investigation lasting forty days, he was convicted of having made war against the British, with abetting rebellion, with proclaiming himself the reigning sovereign of India, and with causing, or being accessory to, the death of many Europeans. He was sentenced to be transported for life, and was sent to Rangoon where he died on November 7th, 1862.

"General" Bakht Khān was much sought for after the mutiny but was never found or heard of. He does not appear to have been killed. He was an artillery *ṣūbedār* of a famous field battery and had served with it at Jalalabad under Sale in the first Afghān war. The battery had a mural crown as an honorary decoration on their guns.

Archaeological work carried out in Delhi Fort.

Previous to the year 1903 the historical buildings, of the Fort at Delhi and their immediate surroundings were in the most neglected and unsatisfactory condition. Many of them were sadly in need of repair, others were used as barrack rooms or stores, while the area in which they stood was cut up by modern roads, and disfigured by unsightly military buildings. Old levels were obliterated, and the disheartened visitor to the former Palace of the "Great Moghul" wandered aimlessly about from building to building. Seen under these conditions, the place lost much of its interest and it was impossible for the average visitor to revisualise its former condition. The associations of the Fort, its place in history and architecture demanded that something should be done, and the gardens as they now stand together with the conservation of the buildings in the area, are the outcome of the improvements suggested by the Director General of Archæology in 1902. These suggestions embodied the acquisition from the military authorities of as much of the old area formerly occupied by the Palace as was possible, so that it might be enclosed and kept in a state of orderliness, and the buildings it contained secured from further molestation or damage. This done, the ground was to be reduced as far as was possible to its old levels, the modern buildings and roads removed, and the area was to be laid out in lawns and shrubberies so that the buildings might be seen under more happy conditions.

The lawns and shrubberies were to represent respectively the position of former courtyards and buildings which had been removed, but whose position was traceable by the help of their buried foundations and old plans. In the case of the northern portion of the area—the Ḥayāt Bakhsh garden, where vestiges of the old water channels and causeways were abundant, but buried under three feet of earth and rubbish—the fact that the gardens would be eventually used for occasions such as the Royal Garden Party held during the recent Durbar, necessitated more reconstructive work, so that the old channels and fountains could be made to fulfil their former functions. It must not be imagined that, small though the area may appear to many, all this has been accomplished with a sweep of the pen. Till 1908 work was going on slowly, and its completion would have taken many more years had it not been that the Coronation Durbar created a demand that the buildings, which had so many years before witnessed the similar ceremonies of the "Great Moghul," should be seen under more ideal conditions.

The evacuation of the ground by the military authorities, the preparation of new buildings to take the place of those removed outside the area, and the difficulties of irrigation owing to the danger of mosquitoes breeding in water standing in the gardens had all to be arranged for, before the scheme could be successfully brought to a conclusion.

In 1904-05 excavations were made on a large scale in the Ḥayāt Ba<u>khsh</u> garden which laid bare the ancient tanks and water channels. The extent of the large tank, of which the Ẓafar Maḥal is the central feature, was also determined. In 1905-06 the work was continued, and a start was made on the reconstruction of the old channels. Fragments of the ornamental kerb and cause-ways were found between the tank and the "Sāwan" pavilion, and from these, together with the old plans, which showed the border, it was possible to carry out the work with certainty. The large central tank, built by <u>Sh</u>āhjahān, appears to have been deepened, probably at the same time as the Ẓafar Maḥal was erected in its centre, and this had been done by building a parapet on the top of the ornamental border. Had this parapet been added by the British the course would have been obvious, but it bore elaborate surroundings and was obviously Mughal work. Accordingly it was felt that the traces of the parapet's existence should not be destroyed, and the missing portions of it have been therefore restored so that the tank can be filled up to the higher level.

The parapet round the tank was completed in 1906-07, while the construction of the four main causeways with their channels, pavements and ornamental beds was proceeded with. They were completed in 1907-08, and during the excavation traces of subsidiary channels were discovered, dividing each quarter of the garden into four equal squares. The clearance of the entire site was not attempted until 1908-09, there being difficulties in finding a place to dump the spoil earth taken from the works. Further excavations revealed a pathway on the east side of the garden connecting the north and south pathways. Part of this only was repaired at first, the remainder being completed when the battery and military road to it on the east terrace were removed in 1913. It was a pity that the site could not be lowered to its original level in the first instance, as the sides of the channels, after they were dug out, were found to be in a *kachcha* condition and needing considerable repairs. In the summer of 1908, a conference was held at Simla at which the Director-General of Archæology and representative military authorities were present, and among other important points, it was decided that the tank and channels the Ḥayāt Bakhsh garden could be filled between 1st December and 31st March,[1] servants' quarters within the archæological area demolished, and that the Naubat Khāna, the Shāh Burj and the Mumtāz Mahal could be included in the area.

In 1909-10 substantial progress was made in the work on the gardens, and the iron railings round the area were practically complete. The main entrance to the garden was fixed through the Naubat Khāna, thereby reviving the old Mughal custom; for it was at this point that all visitors to the court descended from their palanquins or elephants and approached the Royal presence on foot; while one private entrance was provided to the south of the Dīwān-i-'Āmm and a special military entrance near the Shāh Burj, so that access could be gained to the battery on the east terrace. In the Ḥayāt Bakhsh garden the work on the minor intersecting causeways with their water channels had been completed, and the whole of the area of this garden had been lowered to its original level and dressed ready for grass. At the end of the year the work on the water supply which now irrigates the whole garden was well in hand. The water is raised up from two old wells, one of which is outside the area on the barrack square, into reinforced concrete tanks behind the "Bhādon" pavilion, by means of two electrically driven pumps.

The buildings within the area have, since 1902, all been thoroughly repaired. The work on the mosaics in the Dīwān-i-'Āmm has already been referred to,

[1] It has unfortunately been found impossible to arrange for this owing to danger of malaria.

while modern additions have been removed from the Naubat Khāna, Rang Maḥal and Mumtāz Maḥal, and these buildings restored, as far as compatible with the precepts of archæological conservation, to their former appearance. The Shāh Burj pavilion which was, in 1904, in imminent danger of falling has been permanently secured, while the pavilions of the Ḥayāt Bakhsh garden have been thoroughly overhauled, and their marble tanks and cascades revealed.

In 1910-11 the Ḥayāt Bakhsh garden was grassed and planted. The positions of the old buildings are indicated by masses of flowering shrubs, while a screen of conifers, backed by *grevillea* trees, masks the iron railings and barracks surrounding the area. With the exception of the east terrace the garden was now complete, and it was easy to see that the whole area, when treated on these lines, gave abundant promise of future charm. Early in January 1911 Sir John Hewett with the Durbar Committee had visited the gardens, and it was decided that a Royal garden party should be held there at the time of the Coronation Durbar, and that the rest of the area should be laid out immediately, in accordance with the scheme of the Archæological Department. The most difficult part of the work remaining to be done was the trenching for the shrubberies and lawns. The débris of old buildings and roads had to be removed and suitable earth provided. The large tank between the Rang Maḥal and the Diwān-i-'Āmm which had been filled up and crossed by a military road and a drain, was excavated. Traces were found in its centre of a little square building with a central tank, probably designed on the same lines as the Ẓafar Maḥal in the Ḥayāt Ba<u>kh</u>s<u>h</u> garden, and reached by a little causeway, the bases of the piers of which were found *in situ*. These, with what remained of the building, have been carefully preserved. It has not been possible hitherto to provide sufficient water for this tank so the bottom has been grassed. Some of the old coping stones were found in position, and an old stone ring was found, built in one corner of the tank, which points to the probability of its having been screened on occasion from the sun by a *<u>sh</u>āmiyāna* (sunawning).

The marble basin, originally belonging to the Fort, but which had found its way into the Queen's gardens in the city (see page 18) was brought back and has been placed in the centre of the little platform in this tank. Old pictures clearly show this basin placed in front of the Rang Maḥal, but how far from it is difficult to judge; it has consequently been placed here as being as near its old position as could be determined with accuracy.

The paths have been laid down so as to follow as far as possible their old lines. The inner and outer courts in front of the Dīwān-i-<u>Kh</u>āṣṣ are represented by lawns and the buildings between them by shrubberies, composed of *Inga* hedges, backed by banks of *Acalephan* and *Duranta*, while behind these again are taller shrubs such as *Murry*, *Hamelia*, *Bougainvillea* (the compact variety), *Hibiscus*, *Tecoma*, etc. It should be added that in trenching for these shrubberies the foundations of the old buildings were found as expected in almost every case.

Grass courts have similarly been formed in front of the Dīwān-i-'Āmm and Mumtāz Maḥal. In the case of the first, the old courtyard that formerly existed in front of it, and which witnessed the daily *darbār* of the Emperor, was lined at either side by *dālāns* or colonnades, as at Agra. All traces of these had vanished and a military road ran between the Naubat Khāna and the Dīwān-i-'Āmm. The old colonnades are now represented by a screen of *grevilleas* and conifers. The line of *grevilleas* to the north of the central pathway occupies almost the same position as the old colonnade, but that to the south is unavoidably nearer to the central pathway owing, as has already been said, to its being impossible to remove the military road which runs outside the new railing.

Another shrubbery runs due north and south from the ends of the Dīwān-i-'Āmm and represents the buildings seen starring from the ends of the Dīwān-i-'Āmm in the old pictures and plans. These buildings screened off the private precincts of the Palace from the public eye.

The grass court in front of the Mumtāz Maḥal is not reduced to its original level as yet, and it will be seen that the plinth of this building is still partially hidden. The fragments of a marble tank were found in front of it through which a water pipe had unfortunately been laid. When this portion of the garden is dealt with, it may be possible to do something to expose the tank in question between the Rang Mahal and the Mumtāz Maḥal. Trenching revealed an underground drain leading to a doorway in the outer wall of the

Fort (see page 7), which had apparently been bricked up by Mughal builders themselves.

The other portion of the garden that still remained to be put in order at the end of 1910 was the east terrace of the Ḥayāt Bakhsh garden. This is raised some 5 feet above the level of the remainder of the garden. There were buildings on it formerly and it was found that a retaining wall ran along its western face. The backing of this was found and has been preserved by Mughal brick facing with recessed pointing. This wall ran from the north wall of the Ḥammām to the Shāh Burj, but it was impossible, at first, to continue its alignment owing to the presence of the gun battery and military road which gave access to it. The removal of the battery has brought to light traces of the pavilion, the Motī Maḥal, that formerly existed here, which is now represented by the large rectangular clump of shrubbery.

Since 1913 the principal work that has been carried out in the Fort has been in connection with the improvement of the Ḥayāt Bakhsh garden and the completion of the restored water-channel and causeways therein; while copper-plated doors of appropriate design were affixed to the openings in the Khāṣṣ Maḥal which had been fitted up in the Mughal manner to enable the visitor to visualise the interior appointments of the period.

The outline of the water-channel named the Nahr-i-Bihisht (Stream of Paradise) disclosed during the excavations in 1910 has since been represented by flower beds. In front of the Hīrā Maḥal was also found a shallow basin with a channel leading westward, evidently to connect up with the minor channel of the Ḥayāt Bakhsh garden which runs into the path near this point; from the character of the work it appeared to be of the late Mughal period. The Nahr-i-Bihisht was provided with fountains at frequent intervals and the copper pipes of several of these were found. After passing along the east terrace in the manner described the water entered the channel in the Ḥammām and so passed on along the outer range of buildings to the Rang Maḥal.

The new water installation, also calls for comment. This, besides providing for the irrigation of the garden and shrubberies, enables the channels of the Ḥayāt Bakhsh garden and the Ẓafar Maḥal tank to be filled. It also provides for the working of the fountains in the Ẓafar Maḥal tank and in the main channels running from the "Sāwan" to the "Bhādon" pavilions, and for the cascades in these two last and in the Shāh Burj. The marble channel from the Hammām to the south end of the Rang Maḥal can also be provided with water, as formerly, while a fountain jet has been fixed in the marble basin in front of the Rang Maḥal.

The amount of water required to operate the fountains and cascades and at the same time to fill the tanks and channels is very considerable, and continuous pumping for about two weeks is necessary. The military authorities at present object to the water standing in the garden and channels unless covered with kerosene to prevent the breeding of mosquitoes. This consideration also forbade the disposal of the water on the ground below the Fort and a scheme has accordingly been prepared by which the water can be raised into the tanks again and so re-used. However, the removal of certain of the military barracks to the immediate west of the Ḥayāt Bakhsh garden has been hinted at, so it is hoped that these difficulties may be eventually overcome and that the fountains and tanks may be permanently provided with water during the cold season and not for important ceremonial occasions only, as at present. The additional charm the sheets of water give to the buildings and gardens cannot be overestimated.

The removal of the barracks to the west of the Ḥayāt Bakhsh garden would also enable its western portion to be completed, together with the Mahtāb Bāgh, a work which would greatly enhance the charm of the Fort. The acquisition of the strip of ground between the Mumtāz Maḥal and the Asad Burj has also been suggested to the authorities, so that the whole of the east terrace of the Fort, from north to south, may be open to visitors.

The accompanying table shows the amount spent annually on repairs and improvements to the Fort, since 1883-84 :—

	Rs.	A.	P.
1883-84	2,226	0	0
1884-85	6,842	0	0
1885-86	599	0	0
1886-87	8,037	0	0
1887-88	4,645	0	0
1888-89	..		
1889-90	..		
1890-91	3,519	0	0
1891-92	1,230	0	0
1892-93	1,350	0	0
Carried over	28,448	0	0

	Rs.	A.	P.
Brought forward	28,448	0	0
1893-94	1,689	0	0
1894-95	525	0	0
1895-96	731	0	0
1896-97	517	0	0
1897-98	1,760	0	0
1898-99	..		
1899-1900	..		
1900-01	543	0	0
1901-02	509	0	0
1902-03	700	0	0
1903-04	19,123	0	0
1904-05	10,452	0	0
1905-06	26,663	0	0
1906-07	8,106	0	0
1907-08	10,201	0	0
1908-09	34,813	0	0
1909-10	20,092	0	0
1910-11	26,948	0	0
1911-12 (Coronation Durbar year)	81,240	0	0
1912-13	4,881	0	0
1913-14	9,094	0	0
1914-15	6,935	0	0
1915-16	2,747	0	0
1916-17	2,200	0	0
1917-18	1,100	0	0
1918-19	1,100	0	0
1919-20	1,100	0	0
1920-21	1,100	0	0
1921-22	1,100	0	0
1922-23	1,184	0	0
1923-24	1,867	0	0
1924-25	1,008	0	0
1925-26	1,005	0	0
1926-27	2,948	0	0
1927-28	1,228	0	0
1928-29	1,415	0	0
1929-30	852	0	0
1930-31	2,866	0	0
1931-32	1,915	0	0
1932-33	525	0	0
1933-34	3,948	0	0
1934-35	1,562	0	0
1935-36	1,691	0	0
TOTAL	3,28,431	0	0

MGIPC—M—III-9-21—9-3-37—2,000.

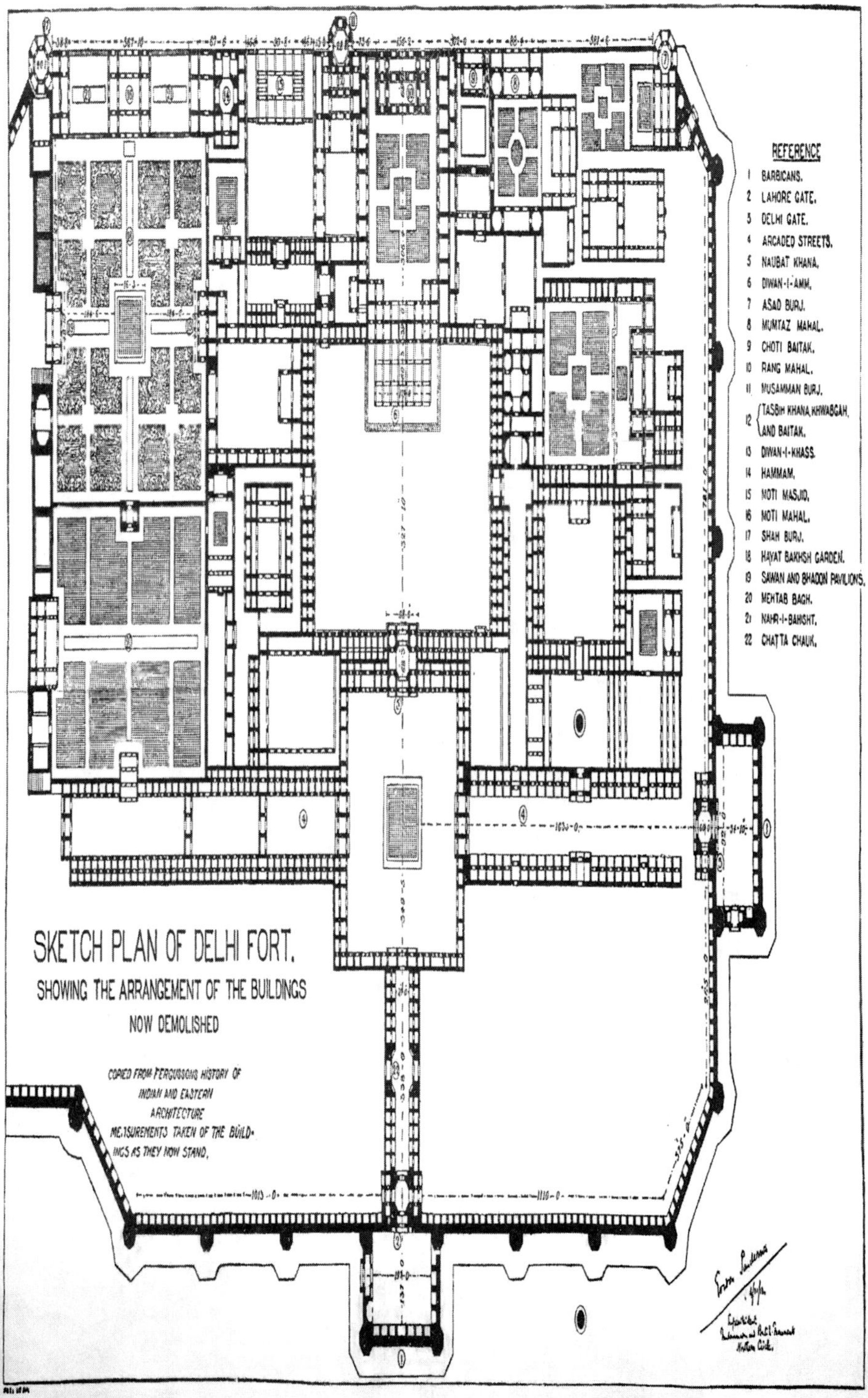

SKETCH PLAN OF DELHI FORT.
SHOWING THE ARRANGEMENT OF THE BUILDINGS
NOW DEMOLISHED
COPIED FROM FERGUSSONS HISTORY OF
INDIAN AND EASTERN
ARCHITECTURE
MEASUREMENTS TAKEN OF THE BUILD-
INGS AS THEY NOW STAND.
REFERENCE
1 BARBICANS.
2 LAHORE GATE.
3 DELHI GATE.
4 ARCADED STREETS.
5 NAUBAT KHANA.
6 DIWAN-I-AMM.
7 ASAD BURJ.
8 MUMTAZ MAHAL.
9 CHOTI BAITAK.
10 RANG MAHAL.
11 MUSAMMAN BURJ.
12 TASBIH KHANA, KHWABGAH, AND BAITAK.
13 DIWAN-I-KHASS.
14 HAMMAM.
15 MOTI MASJID.
16 MOTI MAHAL.
17 SHAH BURJ.
18 HAYAT BAKHSH GARDEN.
19 SAWAN AND BHADON PAVILIONS.
20 MEHTAB BAGH.
21 NAHR-I-BAHISHT.
22 CHATTA CHAUK.

THE CITADEL OF THE "GREAT MOGHUL" DELHI
BUILT BY SHAHJAHAN 1638-1648, AND ADDED TO BY AURANGZEB
REFERENCE
1. SALIMGARH
2. BRIDGE BUILT BY JAHANGIR
3. SHAH BURJ
4. MOTI MAHAL
5. HAMMAM
6. DIWAN-I-KHAS
7. KHWABGAH & JHAROKA
8. RANG MAHAL
9. RIVER JAMNA
10 MUMTAZ MAHAL
11. DIWAN-I-AMM
12 NAUBAT KHANA
13 TANK
14 ARCADED STREET
15. ASAD BURJ
16 CITY WALL
17 MOAT
18 DELHI GATE
19 BARBICANS BUILT BY AURANGZEB
20 LAHORE GATE
21 COVERED BAZAR
22 ARCADED STREET
23 BHADON PAVILION
24 SAWAN PAVILION
25 MOTI MASJID BUILT BY AURANGZEB
26 HAYAT BAKHSH GARDEN
27 GARDEN OF MOONLIGHT